An Introduction to Travel and Tourism

John Ward

Pearson Education Limited
Edinburgh Gate
Harlow
Essex CM20 2JE, England
and Associated Companies throughout the world

First published 2000
Reprinted 2001

ISBN 0 582 41909-3

British Library Cataloguing-in-Publication Data

A catalogue record for this book is available from the British Library.

Set by 3 in Humanist, Rotis Serif, Caslon
Produced by Pearson Education Asia Pte Ltd
Printed in Singapore (KKP)

Acknowledgements

The author and publishers are grateful to the following for permission to
reproduce copyright material:

The Countryside Agency; The Forestry Commission; The National Trust;
The National Trust Photo Library; P & O Cruises; The Travel Training
Company

Also available

Ward – *Introduction to Travel and Tourism Support Pack*
ISBN 0-582-41910-7

Contents

Modules for GCSE Travel and Tourism

Module 1   Researching a tourist destination

Module 2 Investigating a leisure facility

MODULES FOR GCSE TRAVEL AND TOURISM

Module 3   Social, cultural and environmental impact of tourism

Module 4   Employment in the tourism industry

Introduction

After the publication of the case study book, *GCSE Travel and Tourism*, many teachers began to say that they would like to see a complementary text, using an activity-based approach. Many expressed concerns about the reading level of their students, suggesting that there was considerable demand for texts which would be easier to read. This book is a response to those views.

The book will primarily be of interest to teachers and students of GCSE Travel and Tourism, though there are many areas of the content which will also make it an appropriate resource for GNVQ Foundation and Intermediate Leisure and Tourism, as well as GNVQ Part One.

The book is divided into six chapters:

- **What is tourism?**
- **Planning a holiday**
- **Choosing where to go**
- **Providing tourism products and services**
- **Working in travel and tourism**
- **Do people and places benefit from tourism?**

The opening chapter uses Activities and Exercises to help students define key areas of tourism and understand the various components of the industry. Chapter 2 encourages them to think about the processes of choosing a holiday while Chapter 3 identifies the characteristics of different types of tourist destination. Chapter 4 focuses on products and services and provides an overview of the operation of leisure facilities. Chapter 5 helps students to understand issues relating to working in travel and tourism, as well as the basic process of applying for jobs. Chapter 6 puts tourism in a wider context by asking students to consider the actual and potential impacts which tourism has on host communities and environments.

There are over 100 Activities and Exercises in the book. Exercises are simpler tasks of checking recall or understanding of terms whereas Activities require research and lead to extended writing, planning, designing or discussion work. Students are asked to complete tables, write reports and letters, design posters, discuss issues, take part in role plays and find out further information. Many Activities and Exercises begin with straightforward tasks which can be completed in class and go on to extension Activities which can be set as homework.

You may wish to warn students not to write on the text. Boxes and blanks in the Activities and Exercises should be copied for students' own work.

The matrix on pp. ix–xii shows where elements of the GCSE Travel and Tourism syllabus are covered in the book.

What is tourism?

Which people are tourists?

Some people would say a tourist is a person on holiday.

Tourists on a beach

Exercise 1.1

Tick the spaces in the table below to show which of the statements you think are true about **all** tourists, **some** tourists or **no** tourists.

	True about all tourists	True about some tourists	True about no tourists
they are away from home			
they are enjoying themselves			
they are in a foreign country			
they are spending money			
they are visiting friends			
they are staying at least one night in the place they are visiting			
they mean to return home in the near future			
they are on business			
they are with their family			

Use the statements you have ticked in column one (**True about all tourists**) to write down what you think a tourist is:

A tourist is ...

Did you find it difficult to decide where to place some of your ticks? Why was this?

Here is a definition which is often used by people collecting information about tourists and their activities:

'Tourists are temporary visitors staying at least 24 hours in the country visited for leisure, business, family visits or meetings.'

Why do people travel?

Another way of explaining who tourists are is to look at *why* they go from one place to another.

Exercise 1.2

Column **A** in the table below shows some different reasons for travelling. Column **B** gives some examples of people who are travelling.

Can you match up each traveller in Column B with one of the reasons for travelling in Column A?

A *Reason for travelling*	B *Example of a traveller*	C
1 to have a rest from work	**a** Mr Ivor Payne goes to America for a heart operation	
2 to visit some friends or relatives	**b** Miss Wanda Cook goes to Paris to train to be a chef	
3 to meet some business customers	**c** Mr Chris Chan goes to Rome to hear the Pope's Easter message	
4 to study for a qualification	**d** Mr Andy Player goes to France to watch the football World Cup	
5 to get some special hospital treatment	**e** Mr Ray Sloane goes to Hong Kong to open a new office for his company	
6 to visit an important religious place	**f** Ms Honour Brake goes to Spain for a week's holiday	
7 to go to an important event	**g** Mrs May Kerpall goes to Germany to stay with her brother	

List an example of your own in Column C for each of the seven reasons for travelling given in Column A

So tourists may be doing more than just having a holiday. They may be combining two or more things like visiting friends and attending an exhibition they are interested in.

People travel for different reasons

Does it matter who we count as tourists?

Think about the three examples below:

1   **The number of cars being driven into Brighton on summer weekends**

2   **The amount of money spent by visitors to Ibiza in August**

3   **The number of extra jobs which might be created in Tobago if permission was granted to build three new hotels**

Who might want to know?

In example 1 the local authority in Brighton might want to know. It would help them to plan ways of dealing with heavy traffic and parking problems.

In example 2 the tourism industry on the island might want to know. They could use the information to show that tourism was important in bringing money to the island. It would help them to get government support for new tourism developments like hotels or new roads.

In example 3 the government of Tobago might want to know. It would help them to show that their policy of agreeing to hotel development was for the good of the local people.

In each case the *total* numbers would be important, but in example 1 it would be difficult to tell how many of the total were:

- ✪ **Holiday makers**
- ✪ **Business travellers**
- ✪ **Local people**

In examples 2 and 3 it would be difficult to tell how much of the spending was done by each of these groups or how much each of the three groups would be likely to use the hotels. It is easier to count all of these groups as tourists, as long as they are travelling and using the same facilities like hotels.

Tourism – true or false?

Exercise 1.3

Tick the boxes in the table below to show whether you think each of the statements is true or false:

Statement	True	False
1 All visitors to Spain are going on holiday		
2 Football fans going to see their team play abroad sometimes use the same facilities as holiday-makers		
3 Tourists have to be visiting a foreign country		
4 A person who works overseas for three years is a tourist		
5 Tourists include anyone who uses an airline and a hotel on the same journey		
6 Tourists spend money in local shops		
7 People in Britain only go on holiday in the summer months		
8 Different countries like to know how many visitors they are getting		
9 Many explanations of what a tourist is do not include people going out for day trips		
10 Tourism can create extra jobs for people		

continued

continued

Your answers will help in working out what you have learnt about tourism and tourists so far. See if your answers agree with those below:

1 **False** – some visitors to Spain will be going on business, to stay with relatives or even, if they live near the border, to go shopping or to work.

2 **True** – they may stay in the same hotels, buy things from the same shops, use the same local trains and buses.

3 **False** – a family from London on a two week holiday in Cornwall would still be counted as tourists.

4 **False** – someone working abroad for that length of time would be thought of as if they were a resident of the country they were living in.

5 **True** – tourists use transport (airlines, buses, cars, ferries, taxis etc), accommodation (hotels, apartments, camp sites etc), catering (restaurants, bars, ice creams etc), attractions (theme parks, museums, galleries etc) and services (guides, currency exchange, information centres etc).

6 **True** – tourists buy souvenirs, photographic film, food, maps and many other things which can help to keep shops in business.

7 **False** – more and more people are taking short breaks, especially in the Spring and Autumn. For example, these might be to visit interesting cities or to take part in activities like riding or sailing.

8 **True** – this helps them to decide how to plan so that tourists enjoy their stay and are not put off by crowds or facilities which are not good enough for the number of people using them. It also helps them to persuade people to invest money in providing new facilities.

9 **True** – although people going on day trips do have some things in common with tourists. For example they visit attractions and spend money in shops. People on day trips are sometimes called *excursionists*.

10 **True** – if tourism increases in a place so does the amount of money they spend. This often means that people can start up new businesses. For example they might sell souvenirs to tourists, or sell local food supplies to new hotels, or set up a taxi service.

Discuss the ten statements and see if you can think up other examples to show you understand each of the ten answers.

What is the tourism industry?

Let's begin by looking at some things which we can say about all industries:

They are made up of many different businesses, large and small

These businesses need money to get themselves established

They design and make products and services

They find ways of letting people know about these products and services

They find ways of making them available to people who are interested in them

They sell the products and services to their customers

They provide employment for people

Varied facilities for tourists

Exercise 1.4

For the tourism industry complete the statements in the table below:

1 An example of a large tourism business is	
2 An example of a small tourism business is	
3 A small tourism business could raise money to get started by	
4 An example of a tourism product is	
5 An example of a tourism service is	
6 A tourism business could let people know about one of its products by	
7 A tourism business could make a product available to people by	
8 An example of selling a tourism product or service is	
9 A tourism business may employ people to	

See how your answers compare with the examples given below:

1 British Airways; Thomson Holidays; Forte Hotels (Granada); American Express.

2 A deckchair seller; an ice cream van; a seafront cafe; a market souvenir stall.

3 Borrowing money from the bank; selling assets such as a house; getting a government grant.

4 A package holiday; an airline ticket; a beginners' sailing course.

5 Providing tourist information; exchanging currency; providing a free bus service from the hotel to the beach.

6 Advertising; direct mail; recommendations of customers.

7 Having its brochures in a travel agency; letting people book a room or flight through the internet; putting advertisements with booking forms in newspapers.

continued

continued

8 Taking a booking for a flight or a holiday; selling a stick of rock; hiring a guide.

9 Wait at tables; repair theme park rides; fly an aeroplane; teach people how to windsurf.

There are plenty of other examples. When you put them all together you begin to get the idea that tourism is a very large industry in which many different products and services are supplied to customers.

To understand the tourism industry better we need to see how it can be broken down into different parts.

Activity 1.1

Think of a holiday you went on. Make a list of all the things you did which depended on somebody else doing their job.

Here is an example

What I did . . .	Who it depended on . . .
Booked a holiday on a Greek island	My local travel agent
Went to the airport	A minicab firm
Flew to Athens	A charter airline
Travelled to the island of Skopelos	Greek ferry company
Stayed for 2 weeks	The Aghia Galini Hotel
Had meals out	Various local restaurants and tavernas
Went on a boat trip	Ianni, a local fisherman
Bought postcards and a bottle of ouzo	The village shop

Greek island holiday

Is the example of the Greek holiday the same as your own example in any ways?

We could say it tells us the following things about the tourism industry:

- **Some of the businesses in it are small, perhaps run by just one or two people**

- **Others have offices and facilities all over the world, like international airlines**

- **Transport, accommodation and catering are important parts of the tourism industry**

- **There are many businesses, such as shops or taxi firms, which are used partly by tourists and partly by local people**

- **Many people are employed in the industry, carrying out a wide range of different duties**

Figure 1.1 shows some of the different parts of the tourism industry. These are often called *sectors*.

Let's look at each of these sectors in turn.

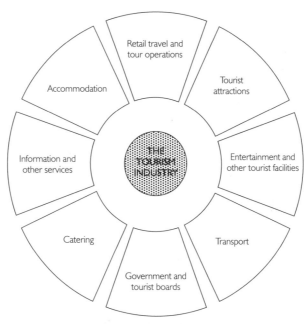

Figure 1.1 The parts of the tourism industry

Which sector of the tourism industry do each of the following work in?

a. theme park safety officer   **e.** local authority tourism officer

b. tour guide   **f.** caravan site manager

c. bingo caller   **g.** travel agent

d. chef   **h.** airline pilot

Accommodation

As we have already seen, tourists spend more than 24 hours in a place away from home. This means they need somewhere to:

✪ **Sleep**

✪ **Store their luggage**

✪ **Relax**

✪ **Eat**

In other words they need somewhere to stay. They can choose from a number of different types of accommodation, such as the ones shown in the following table:

Type of accommodation	Description
hotel	Hotels usually provide rooms to sleep in, meals on full board or half board and sometimes leisure facilities
guest house	A guest house is usually a small house with rooms to sleep in and often a bed and breakfast service
apartment	An apartment is a living and sleeping area, usually in a block. It usually has kitchen and shower facilities
villa	A villa is usually a detached building with kitchen, bathroom and sleeping facilities, often surrounded by private land and sometimes with a swimming pool
chalet	A chalet is a detached unit, often made of materials like wood, with similar self-catering and shower facilities to an apartment
caravan	A caravan has similar facilities to a chalet but generally has wheels so that it can be moved to a different site
tent	Tents are usually canvas and can be either carried by tourists or else set up on site by the owners of a camp site. Facilities are often in a central block which all people on the camp site can use
cruise ship	People on cruise ships sleep in cabins with bathrooms. Meals, leisure facilities and entertainments are provided for everyone on the ship

Holiday accommodation

How can we group different types of accommodation?

Tourist accommodation can be divided into places which provide food and services like cleaning, portering and child-minding and those in which visitors have to do these things themselves.

Accommodation in which food and things like cleaning are provided is called **serviced** accommodation.

Where people do these things for themselves the accommodation is called **self-catering** accommodation.

Figure 1.2 shows the difference:

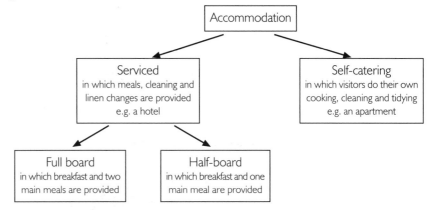

Figure 1.2 Serviced and self-catering accommodation

Exercise 1.6

Listed below are five other kinds of accommodation. Write in the spaces what sort of accommodation you think each one has and how it is different from other types of accommodation.

Accommodation	Your description of it
motel	
pub	
youth hostel	
motorhome	
time share apartment	

How can you tell what the accommodation will be like?

If you are going to stay in any kind of accommodation you will probably want to know:

- ✪ **How to get there**
- ✪ **How much it will cost**
- ✪ **Whether there will be enough room**
- ✪ **How comfortable it is**
- ✪ **How far away it is from places you want to spend time in**
- ✪ **Whether it is near facilities like shops and swimming pools**

If the accommodation is overseas, you might find out what it is like by reading a holiday *brochure* or by asking the *travel agent* where you booked your holiday.

To help people travelling in Britain who want to book their accommodation as they go there are several grading schemes:

Graded accommodation

Crown scheme   Serviced accommodation, like hotels, can be awarded up to five crowns to show what kind of facilities and services they offer.

Key scheme   The number of keys awarded shows what sort of facilities and equipment are available in self-catering apartments.

Q scheme   This scheme tells you what facilities and services are available in holiday caravan, chalet and camping parks.

Moon scheme   This is a scheme like the Crown scheme but for 'bedroom only' establishments which do not provide meals or public rooms.

Accessible scheme   This scheme tells people with disabilities whether they will be able to get proper access to the accommodation.

Activity 1.2

Look in some holiday brochures which include hotels which belong to the Crown classification scheme. Then fill in the following table:

Name of hotel	No of crowns	Facilities and services offered	Cost
	5		
	4		
	3		
	2		
	1		

Which of the hotels in your table would best suit each of these three tourists:

1   Owen Cash, a young trainee chef on a low income, staying overnight in the region before attending an interview the following day.

continued

continued

2   Erna Fortune, Managing Director of Fortune Investments, carrying out some research in the area to enable the company to open a new office.

3   Zena Double, looking for a suitable place for a reunion with the twin sister she has not seen for 20 years.

Explain your choices.

Transport

If a tourist is going to spend more than 24 hours in a place away from home he or she has to have some method of getting to the place they are going (their *destination*) and returning home again. They may also need a means of travelling around while they are in the destination.

People usually travel by means of one of four transport systems:

✪ **Road (e.g. bus, car, coach, taxi)**

✪ **Rail (e.g. train, tram)**

✪ **Air (e.g. jet aircraft, helicopter)**

✪ **Sea (ferry, cruise ship, yacht)**

Transport

Tourists often use a combination of these. For example a holidaymaker might take a taxi to the airport, fly to an overseas destination and travel to a hotel in a coach provided by the holiday company.

Activity 1.3

You will need an atlas and a UK road map for this activity.

Which of the four transport systems could you choose to use for the longest part of the following journeys and why?

From ...	To ...	I would use ...	Because ...
1 London	Sydney		
2 Dover	Calais		
3 Chester	Lincoln		
4 London	Paris		
5 Leeds	Bradford		
6 Bury	Manchester		

For each of these six journeys say which other form of transport you could have used for the longest distance. Give a reason why this was not your first choice of transport to use.

I could have used ...	But the disadvantage would be that ...
1	
2	
3	
4	
5	
6	

Let's have a look at some of things which may have affected your choices in Activity 1.3.

Time and distance

Most people would choose to fly from London to Sydney because it is such a long journey. It takes 20 hours or so to fly. People used to do the journey on passenger ships but it took about 3 weeks to get there. People are often happier to use slower forms of transport on shorter journeys, such as the one from Dover to Calais.

Cost

On some journeys the time it takes to complete the whole journey may be similar using different types of transport. For example there is not much difference in the time taken to travel from the centre of London to the centre of Paris using mainly rail or mainly airline services. This situation means that travellers are more likely to compare the cost and the comfort of the different ways of getting there. Some forms of transport, for example coaches, are often used by travellers wishing to save money.

Comfort

People who are going on holiday may choose a transport system for comfort. It is not just a matter of comfortable seats. They may choose buses because

Comfort and service on an aeroplane

they find driving in traffic stressful. They may be afraid of flying or suffer from sea sickness. They may want to travel directly to their destination, without having to carry their luggage from one transport system to another.

Frequency of services

Some travellers, especially people who are on business, have to arrive at their destination at an exact time, perhaps so that they can go to meetings. This means they will choose the form of transport which has enough services to get them there at the right time of day. If they are travelling a long way and want to fly, the times of services offered by different airlines will help them to choose who they will go with.

Availability of services

You can't choose to travel from Chester to Lincoln by tram because there isn't a tram service available between these two cities. A transport company has to think about a number of things before deciding whether to offer a service between two destinations:

- ✪ **Whether research shows people are asking for this service**
- ✪ **What other services run on the same route**
- ✪ **Whether the company has the machinery and people to run the service**
- ✪ **Whether the service will make a profit**

Types of tourism transport

Some forms of transport are particularly important to tourism. For example an increase in the number of charter flights has meant that more holiday destinations can be reached in less time. Some kinds of tourism, such as a coach tour or a cruise, use transport to visit a number of different places on the same trip. More holiday-makers hire cars now, so that they can visit the areas surrounding their main destination.

Table 1.1 shows the main types of transport and the part they play in the tourism industry.

By ...		Means of transport	Main function
Land	Rail	Express/Inter-City	fast services linking main population centres
		Local	regional, often less frequent services
		Underground/Metro	linking major city centres with outlying districts
		Light railway	often linking other networks, e.g. from airport to rail station
		Tram	system reducing traffic congestion in city centres
	Road	Car/car hire	allows individual control of route and speed
		Coach	inexpensive and able to reach more destinations than rail
		Bus	scheduled services used by visitors and locals alike
		Taxi	fast and convenient for short journeys or transfers
Sea	Ocean/channel	Ferry/hovercraft/hydrofoil	scheduled services linking islands with mainland or crossing channels
		Liner	large ocean-going luxury ships mostly used for cruises
		Cruise ship	follow planned itineraries stopping at places of interest
	River/lake/canal	narrow boat	former working boats converted to accommodate holidaymakers cruising canals
		cabin cruiser	modern motorised boats with accommodation and cooking facilities
		yacht	for sailing holidays; can have accommodation and cooking facilities
Air	Longer flights	jet aircraft	the most rapid means of covering long distances, but relying on good links with other transport systems
	Shorter flights/ sightseeing	helicopter/light aircraft hot air balloon	dependent on take off and landing space; affords 'bird's eye view'

Table 1.1

Activity 1.4

1 Pick **three** examples of means of transport listed in Table 1.1 (e.g. yacht, taxi, helicopter) and describe the sort of person you think might use it for journeys in Europe.

Plot the routes they might take onto a map of Europe.

2 Can you think of any other examples of types of transport not mentioned in the table (e.g. cable car)?

How and where do you think tourists would use these?

Transport links

Because many journeys depend on more than one form of transport, the links between transport systems are important.

Think about the following journey:

Cara Train is travelling from Ireland and plans to meet her cousin, Katya, in London. From there they are going to the South of France for a summer holiday (Table 1.2). Figure 1.3 shows the route which Cara means to follow.

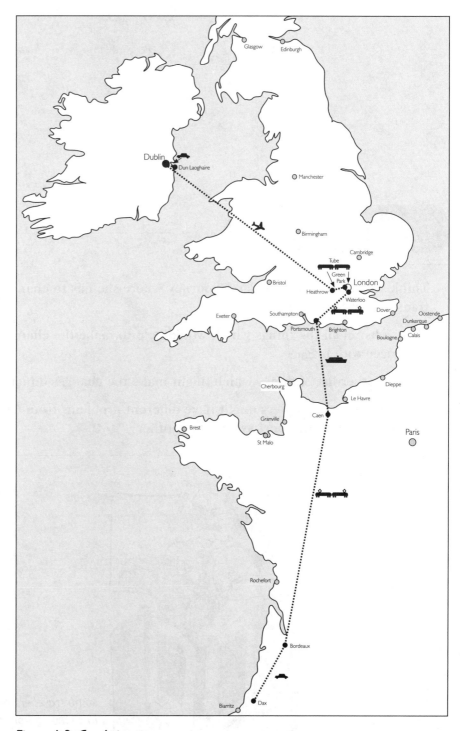

Figure 1.3 Cara's journey

From ...	To ...	Using ...
Dun Laoghaire	Dublin	mini cab
Dublin	Heathrow	air
Heathrow	Green Park	underground – Piccadilly Line
Green Park	Waterloo	underground – Jubilee Line
Waterloo	Portsmouth	rail
Portsmouth	Caen	ferry
Caen	Bordeaux	rail
Bordeaux	Dax	hire car

Table 1.2

Exercise 1.7

Think about the places in Cara's journey where she has to change from one transport system to another.

Make a list of all the things which would help to make the changes easy for a passenger with luggage.

Make another list of things which might make the changes difficult.

Which groups of travellers might have different problems from Cara in changing from one kind of transport system to another?

Some travellers have difficulty in changing from one form of transport to another

Activity 1.5

Draw an outline map of the region you live in.

Mark on it and name:

Your nearest airport

Your nearest main line railway station

Your nearest motorways in and out of the region

Your nearest sea/ferry routes if there are any

Now complete the table below to show what transport people could use to link from one transport system to another.

To get from ...	To ...	They could use ...
the airport	the railway station	
the airport	the motorway	
the railway station	the motorway	
the railway station	the ferry port	
the ferry port	the airport	
the ferry port	the motorway	

Travelling from Britain to Europe

Living on an island means it is more difficult to visit a foreign country than if you only have to cross a border. The same is true for tourists who want to come and visit an island country.

The British travel and tourism industry depends on ferry and air services to transport overseas visitors to Britain and to carry British passengers abroad.

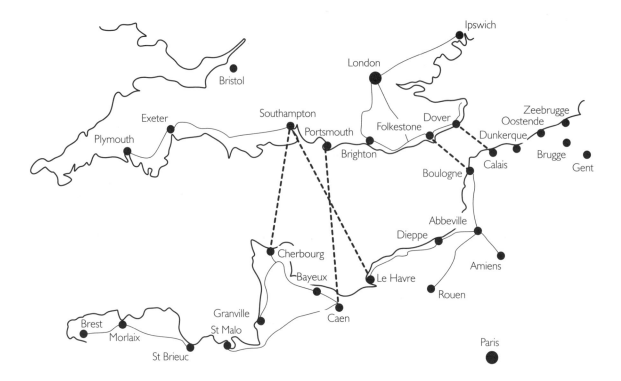

Figure 1.4 Main cross Channel routes

Some facts about cross Channel travel:

- **Three times as many people used cross Channel ferries in 1991 as had done in 1971.**

- **In 1991 5.2 million cars and 182,000 buses and coaches used ferry and hovercraft services across the Channel.**

- **About two thirds of the passengers using ferry services across the Channel head for French ports.**

- **In 1970 61% of people from the UK taking holidays abroad left Britain by plane; by 1994 80% were leaving Britain by plane.**

- **In 1996 3.5 million visits abroad using the Channel Tunnel were made by people living in Britain; 2.7 million visitors to Britain came by this route.**

- **In a 1996 survey over half the travellers returning to Britain through the Channel Tunnel said that they had been on holiday.**

The bar charts in Exercise 1.8 show the numbers of people crossing the Channel to (a) and from (b) Britain and what form of transport they used.

Exercise 1.8

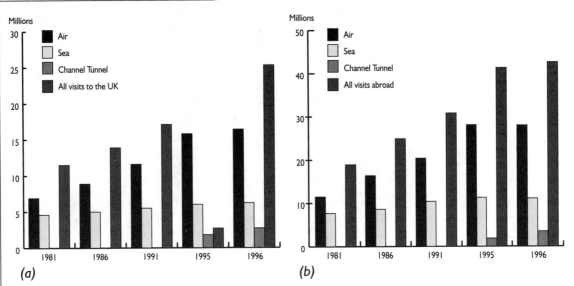

(a)

(b)

Source: *International Passenger Survey, Office for National Statistics*

Look at the bar charts about transport systems used to cross the Channel. Then answer these questions:

1 Is it true that we have more visitors to Britain than we have British people going overseas?

2 Which is the most popular method of crossing the Channel?

3 Compare the number of visits abroad by people from the UK in 1995 and 1996. What differences can you see between the two years?

4 Do the numbers tell you anything about what effect the opening of the Channel Tunnel might be having on the other methods of crossing the Channel?

Catering

An important need which all tourists have is for food and drink. As we have seen some stay in self-catering accommodation, where there are facilities to let them do their own cooking. However, most tourists eat in places like hotels, restaurants, cafes, bars, pubs and fast food outlets.

Table 1.3 samples some of the places where a tourist could choose to eat in a small Spanish resort.

Eating in a restaurant

Place to eat	Type of meals	Cost
hotel	three- and four-course lunches and evening meals, from a set menu or *a la carte*	expensive
restaurant	choice of local dishes, to eat on premises or take away	medium
cafe	'English-style' breakfasts, snacks, sandwiches, cakes and light meals	cheap
fast food outlet	burgers, chips, pizza, baked potatoes, ice cream, salads	cheap
bar	wide range of bar snacks, crisps, peanuts	cheap

Table 1.3

Activity
1.6

Mrs Kerry Oakey has just become the new owner of a small country pub. It is on the border of a National Park and close to a large caravan site.

Local villagers provide most of the customers in the evening. In the daytime the fact that the pub is close to a well-known long distance walk means that some walkers stop there. There is also a small sign on a nearby main road encouraging motorists to turn off and call in at the pub.

continued

Think about who uses the pub now. Also discuss who the new owner might like to encourage to use it more and which groups she might want to keep out.

Mrs Oakey decides to introduce a limited food service.

List the factors which Mrs Oakey would have to think about before adding more choice to the food she was offering in the pub. You could include things like:

★ Whether the ingredients were easy to get

★ How long it would take to cook

★ Whether it would keep

★ Catering for all tastes

Use the grid in Table 1.4 to enter some foods you think she could serve, why these would be suitable, and what effect they would have on the sort of people who come into the pub. One example has already been provided for you.

Name of dish and when available*	This would be suitable because ...	It would affect the sort of people in the pub because ...
e.g. sandwiches (lunchtime)	● Quick to prepare ● Inexpensive	Would attract walkers who may not want a heavy meal before their afternoon's exercise

*For example, at lunch time or in the evening

Table 1.4

Food during travel

Tourists going on longer journeys also need to eat and drink on the way. All of the following are examples of food being provided during the journey:

- ✪ **motorway service areas**
- ✪ **restaurants on cross Channel ferries**
- ✪ **in-flight catering**
- ✪ **railway buffet cars**

Facilities at a motorway service area

Catering for travellers on the move often provides problems for the businesses providing these services. For example:

Type of catering	Problems faced
motorway service areas	• have to stay open long hours • distant from towns so difficult to recruit staff who have to travel
ferry restaurants	• limited time of each crossing • bad weather may cut down number of people choosing to eat
in-flight catering	• not much room to heat and serve food • food has to be prepared, chilled, transported onto planes, and reheated
railway buffet/ restaurant car	• train movements can make serving and eating difficult • passengers may take up two seats – one they reserved and one in the buffet car

Exercise 1.9

Complete the following table to show the kind of catering facilities which each of the tourists described might use.

Explain why you think they would be likely to want this kind of catering.

These tourists ...	Might use ...	Because ...
two American students who have finished university and are on a tour of Europe staying in youth hostels		
the Sales Director of a Japanese car manufacturer in London for some important business meetings		
a couple from Scotland with three children taking 2 weeks' holiday in Cornwall		
an international athlete staying in Portugal to do some outdoor training		
an Indian artist, visiting England for the first time to attend an exhibition of her paintings		
a party of 16-year-olds on a school skiing trip in Switzerland		

Tourist attractions

An attraction is something which makes us want to go and see it.

If you are attracted to a particular place, it usually means that it has either features or facilities which you enjoy. The things that you enjoy may be either *natural* or *human-made*. For example:

Natural features	Human-made features
● beach	● amusement park
● mountains	● swimming pool
● river	● golf course
● lake	● cathedral
● forest	● castle
● cliffs	
● waterfalls	

Visitors enjoying very different attractions

Some human-made attractions may have been built to attract tourists. Others, like castles and cathedrals, only became tourist attractions long after their original use began.

Of course many natural features which attract people, such as beaches, often have built features like piers, amusement parks and promenades added to them. As such places become more popular so the rate of building tends to grow too.

Exercise 1.10

Column **A** of the table below lists a number of different types of tourist attraction.

A Type of tourist attraction	B Example
museum	
cathedral	
theme park	
nature reserve	
historic house	
signposted country walk	
gallery	
boating lake	
castle	
craft shop	

In Column B write down one example of each of the types of attraction given in Column A.

As you can see from Exercise 1.10, each tourist destination will probably contain a number of different tourist attractions. If transport gets the visitors to their destination and accommodation gives them somewhere to stay while they are there, attractions give them some interesting things to do during their stay.

Read the following letter sent by Trev and Ella Longway, who are touring Indonesia, to their friend Norma Leholme.

Dear Norma,

You'd love it out here. When we arrived we went first to Lombok. The beaches were wonderful. Trev remembered to bring his snorkel and the colours of the fish are sensational. We had some great seafood at a restaurant on the edge of the beach.

From Lombok we took a two-day boat trip, taking in Komodo Island. I don't know if you've ever seen pictures of Komodo Dragons? They're huge monitor lizards and grow up to ten or twelve feet long. They look like something out of Jurassic Park! If they bite you you're in real trouble.

We then moved on to Bali which was much busier. You should see the dancing. We went to a show where the dancers performed ancient stories about gods, dragons and people. The costumes were very colourful.

There are some very interesting temples and palaces in Indonesia. We saw the Sultan's Palace in Yogyakarta and two amazing temples at Borobadur and Prambanan. I took lots of photographs.

We spent a couple of days in the East of Java and went on a tour that took us up the rim of a live volcano. We arrived before dawn, just in time to see the sun rise. It was the most amazing view I've ever seen. Trev went very close to the edge but managed not to fall in!

Tomorrow we go back to Jakarta and fly to Hong Kong for a couple of days – Trev wants to go on the hydrofoil to Macau but I'm planning to do lots of shopping!

Look forward to seeing you when we get back,

Love,

Ella

1   Make a list of the tourist attractions which Trev and Ella came across on their trip to Indonesia.

2   How many of these are natural and how many are human-made?

3   Think about the attractions you saw or visited the last time you went on holiday.

   List them and then place them in one of the following categories:

   natural features   *rides and transport*

   entertainments   *shopping*

   sports facilities   *arts and culture*

   places with historic links   *others*

4   Does this tell you anything about the destination you went to or about the kind of visitors you think it is trying to attract?

Retail travel and tour operations

So far we have looked at accommodation, transport and attractions. These are all things which tourists *buy* as part of their holiday or trip.

A very important part of the tourism industry is the businesses which create and sell holidays and other stays away from home. These businesses can be divided into two groups:

✪ **Travel agents**

✪ **Tour operators**

Window of a travel agency

Table 1.5 shows some of the main differences between travel agents and tour operators. It also shows that travel agents and tour operators are involved in selling the products of other companies, such as hotels, airlines and ferry operators (these are sometimes called *principals*), to the public.

The principals develop things like accommodation and transport services which the public can book direct from them. Tour operators put together different services provided by principals into holiday packages. Some of these are sold directly to the public. Many package holidays are sold through travel agents.

A travel agent ...	A tour operator ...
... is often based in a High Street shop	... is usually based in an office
... does not arrange or organise holidays	... puts together different parts of a holiday, often as a package
... puts other companies' brochures on display in the shop	... usually produces brochures advertising holidays they have put together
... sells other companies' holidays and transport tickets over the counter to the public ...	... may sell some holidays by direct telephone or mail bookings from the public
... makes a profit by receiving payment from tour operators or transport companies whose products they sell	... makes a profit by selling holidays, often through travel agents

Table 1.5

The agents advertise the tour operators' products in brochures. They are paid commission by the operators and by accommodation and transport suppliers when they sell their products separately. The commission is based on the amount of each sale they make.

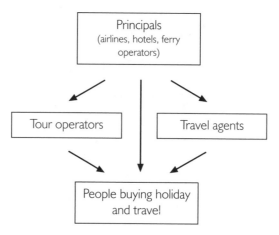

Figure 1.5 How tourism products are sold

Exercise 1.11

You can go into a travel agency and buy a holiday in the same way that you can buy clothes in a shop. However a holiday is a different product from, say, a T-shirt. For example you can't take a holiday home and try it on! You don't know what some parts of it will be like until you set off.

continued

continued

Discuss some of the other ways in which buying a T-shirt is different from buying a holiday.

The following table lists some of the things which happen before or when you buy a T-shirt (Column **A**).

A To sell a T-shirt someone must . . .	B To sell a holiday someone must . . .
create a new design	the person who does this is:
persuade a shop that the design will sell	the person who does this is:
agree a contract to supply them	the person who does this is:
purchase material	the person who does this is:
manufacture the T-shirts	the person who does this is:
deliver them on time to the shop	the person who does this is:
let customers know they are available	the person who does this is:

Write in Column B the things you think are most like the activities in Column A and whether they are done by a principal, a tour operator or a travel agent.

Travel agents

Inside a travel agency

Let's take a look at what a travel agent does. All of the following are activities we might expect them to carry out:

- ✪ **Advise customers about different tourist destinations**

- ✪ **Make available brochures advertising holidays and explain the details contained in them**

- ✪ **Explain the differences between tour operators offering holidays to the same destinations**

- ✪ **Check the availability of particular holidays, flights or ferry crossings**

- ✪ **Work out the cost of different holidays and of extras like car hire, single rooms or travelling at different times**

- ✪ **Sell holiday products and services, including package tours, flight and ferry tickets, holiday insurance and currency exchange**

Not all travel agents deal with the same kind of business. Some aim to provide expert advice and products in particular areas like:

- ✪ **Package holidays**

- ✪ **Cheap flight tickets**

- ✪ **Business travel**

- ✪ **Holidays in particular parts of the world**

Some of the companies which offer package holidays and holidays to specific countries are both tour operators and travel agents. This means they create the holiday package by arranging the transport and accommodation, as well as having travel shops where they sell holidays to the public.

A good example is the Thomson Travel Group, which as Thomson Holidays creates package holidays to a range of destinations and as Lunn Poly owns a chain of High Street travel agencies.

Computer reservations systems

An important part of the travel agent's work involves the use of *computer reservations systems* (*CRS*). These systems allow the agent to check whether holiday products, such as a 2-week holiday with Thomson to Florida or a British Airways flight to Rome, are available for the dates on which the customers want to travel.

The advantages of computer reservations systems are:

- ✪ **They provide quick, accurate information for customers**

- ✪ **Some systems enable immediate bookings to be made and some can issue tickets**

- ✪ They are an easy way of comparing prices

- ✪ They give tour operators and airlines very up-to-date figures of how many holidays or flights are still unsold

- ✪ This means they can offer late deals to try and make sure that all their products are sold before the date they are due to start

Activity 1.8

1 Collect a number of newspapers which carry advertisements for holidays.

2 Find three examples of each of the following:

A company selling package holidays

A company offering cheap flight tickets

A company offering holidays mainly in a single country

3 Using the nine examples you have found, complete the following:

Name of company	Products they are offering for sale	What sort of people might buy them?
1		
2		
3		
4		
5		
6		
7		
8		
9		

4 Discuss why you think business travel agents do not usually advertise in newspapers.

Tour operators

As we have already seen, tour operators put together the different parts of what are called by any of the following terms: **inclusive holidays**; **inclusive tours**; **package holidays**; **package tours**.

All these terms mean that the tour operator arranges transport, accommodation and transfers. They do this by buying flight tickets and hotel rooms in bulk. The tour operator also advertises the packages they have put together by means of brochures and in newspapers and, with larger operators, on television.

The four main types of tour operator in the UK are shown in Table 1.6.

Type of operator	What they do
overseas	they provide package holidays to destinations like Spain and Florida – often for a mass market
domestic	they provide holidays in the UK, such as canal cruises, for people not wishing to go abroad
incoming	they provide package holidays in the UK for visitors coming from abroad
specialist	they provide holidays linked to particular activities, such as cycling, or holidays to less well known destinations

Table 1.6

Activity 1.9

Some other terms often used to describe the products which tour operators put together are:

Short haul – usually used to describe a flight which lasts fewer than 5 hours. It would be used to describe flights to places like Spain or Greece.

Long haul – usually used to describe a flight which lasts longer than 5 hours. It would be used to describe flights to places like Thailand or Australia.

Look through a range of travel brochures.

Work out the travel times it would take to reach 20 or so different destinations.

Plot these on an outline map of the world.

Divide them into long haul and short haul journeys and then list two reasons why people might choose a short haul destination and two reasons why they might choose long haul.

Creating a package holiday

Tour operators have to do much of their work long before people actually go on their holidays, such as:

choose destinations	deciding how easy they are to reach, whether they are attractive, what facilities there are and whether they are safe
plan the size of their operation	working out how many holidays they think they can sell in each destination and what sort of profit they would like to make
arrange accommodation	checking it for availability, quality, safety and closeness to facilities
book flights	reserving well in advance seats on charter flights to airports close to the accommodation
plan transfer services	making sure that passengers can get easily from the airport to the place they are staying in
work out a price	including the cost of transport, accommodation and some profit for the business
train and place resort reps	making sure there is someone in the destination to help tourists with local information and sorting out problems
advertise their holidays	producing brochures, newspaper adverts, special offers, describing products on the internet
sell their holidays	agreeing commission rates with travel agents, setting up a telephone sales team, putting reply forms in adverts

Here are some of the things they have to do after people return home from holiday:

deal with any complaints	answering letters and phone calls, giving compensation where something serious has gone wrong which is their fault
advertise new products to their existing customers	sending letters to holiday-makers who have returned home, encouraging them to try a different destination

Dealing with complaints

Activity 1.10

Choose a country in Europe which receives tourists from the UK.

A tour operator is planning to start a new programme of holidays to the country you have selected.

Discuss each of these questions:

Is this country already popular with UK tourists?

What will be the best means of transport for getting people there?

Will this need any sort of transfers for passengers?

What kind of accommodation do you think the tour operator should provide?

Are holidays in the country you've chosen usually cheap or expensive?

What sort of things do you think people would want to know about this country before they would decide to go on holiday there?

Design a small newspaper advertisement for this tour operator which will get people interested in finding out more about its holidays.

Entertainment

Read through the extracts from the holiday diary of Sandra Joyce below.

Providing things for visitors to do – entertainments – is another part of the tourism industry.

People get bored if they don't have things to do while they are on holiday. Some of these they may plan for themselves. For example they may take a book to read. Other things are provided by people in the destination. For example there might be a festival in which different kinds of music are played.

Monday August 9th

We've arrived! A bumpy landing but once off the plane, it's really hot. Down to the beach for a quick swim and the last of the day's sunshine. Back to the hotel for a quick change and then out for a meal and a few drinks in Fernando's Bar. Falling asleep over a Singapore Sling so back for an early night.

Tuesday August 10th

Wednesday August 11th

Thursday August 12th

Up late after last night's party! Tropical rain – by the bucketful – this morning. Had a go in the hotel gym – exercise bike, treadmill and a few light weights. Hard work but should get me in trim for tonight's disco. Afternoon shopping for clothes.

Friday August 13th

Friday 13th and bad luck again with the weather – very wet. Saw James Bond film in very old, noisy cinema in afternoon. Got back to find local dance troupe performing in hotel lobby – very colourful. Watched a bit of TV in my room – all American satellite channels. Later to Fernando's for a seafood supper.

Saturday August 14th

Sunday August 15th

Took a coach tour of the island. Highlights: wood-carvers at work; tour of spice plantation and factory; museum of island life; boat trip out to reef and first experience of snorkelling (can fish really be so brightly coloured?); the driver's very bad jokes.

Notes

Holiday diary

This kind of activity is often planned to help tourists enjoy their stay, but it also brings in money, either by charging for admission or by attracting more visitors who spend money in shops and restaurants. Some entertainments are planned mainly for local people but are also an added attraction for visitors.

Exercise 1.12

Look again at Sandra's holiday diary.

Make a list of all the things she did which you would count as entertainments.

Complete the following table by writing down an entertainment which you think might be suitable for each of the groups of travellers.

Travellers	Type of entertainment they might enjoy ...
Five women, aged between 20 and 27, on a hen weekend to Dublin.	
An American couple in their 60s on their first visit to England, staying the night in a town near you.	
A couple with three young children on a camping holiday in France.	
A party of secondary school students staying at an outdoor centre in the Peak District.	
Three Japanese business travellers attending a conference in the UK about industry and the environment.	

Ideas might include:

A quiz night

Tenpin bowling

Visiting an art gallery

Taking a hot air balloon flight

Mediaeval pageant in Umbria, Italy

Sports and outdoor activities

Many entertainments take place indoors. However other activities which are popular with tourists take place outside. Some of these are sports:

- ✪ **Golf**

- ✪ **Tennis**

- ✪ **Beach volleyball**

- ✪ **Windsurfing**

- ✪ **Rock climbing**

- ✪ **Sailing**

- ✪ **Scuba diving**

A wide choice of outdoor activities

Others are linked to people's interests:

- ✪ **Bird watching**
- ✪ **Walking**
- ✪ **Painting**
- ✪ **Playing games (e.g. cards, backgammon)**

Exercise 1.13

Your Travel and Tourism group is going on a three-day residential course, staying in a Youth Hostel in a National Park. Part of the programme has already been agreed.

Fill in the gaps in the programme below with activities which you think would be suitable for the group. (The gaps are where it says *Activities to be arranged*.) Think about how much time there is, and what your group will have been doing before and afterwards.

Day One	
10.30–3.30	Travel from school to Hostel by minibus
3.30 p.m.	Arrive at Youth Hostel
5.00–5.30 p.m.	Introductory talk by Hostel Manager
5.30–6.30 p.m.	Activity based on information about YHA
6.30–7.30 p.m.	Evening meal
7.30–9.30 p.m.	**Activities to be arranged**
Day Two	
8.00–8.30 a.m.	Breakfast
8.30–9.00 a.m.	Walk to site of footpath repair work
9.00–10.00 a.m.	Demonstration of repair techniques
10.00–10.30 a.m.	Return walk to Youth Hostel
10.30–12.30 p.m.	**Activities to be arranged**
12.30–1.30 p.m.	Lunch

continued

continued	
1.30–2.00 p.m.	Minibus to National Trust property
2.00–3.30 p.m.	Talk by curator and tour of the property
3.30–4.00 p.m.	Minibus back to Youth Hostel
4.00–6.30 p.m.	*Activities to be arranged*
6.30–7.30 p.m.	Evening meal
7.30–9.30 p.m.	Constructing a raft – team-building exercise
Day Three	
8.00–8.30 a.m.	Breakfast
8.30–9.30 a.m.	Key skills task based on YHA accounts
9.30–10.30 a.m.	*Activities to be arranged*
10.30–12.00	Prepare and make short presentations to Hostel Manager
12.00	Lunch and return to school by minibus

Discuss whether you think this programme of activities would meet the needs of your group.

Apart from the activities you have added, what other changes would you suggest to the programme?

What problems might you have in providing the sorts of entertainment you have suggested?

Other facilities and services for tourists

Tourists need facilities and services from the moment they begin to plan a holiday until the time they get back.

Before they set off they may need to make financial arrangements involving *currency exchange* or *travellers' cheques*. Most will invest in some kind of *insurance* against injury or other disruption to their travels.

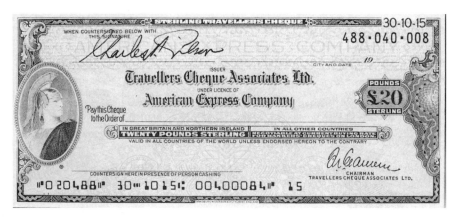

American Express traveller's cheque

Once they have arrived in their chosen destination they will need facilities like *banks*, *shops* and *restaurants*. They may also use *leisure facilities* such as swimming pools or tennis courts. If it is their first visit they will probably call on the services of a *Tourist Information Centre* to find out the most interesting places to visit. They may also take advantage of the services of local *guides* or of *coaches* qualified to teach skills such as canoeing or windsurfing.

What is the difference between a facility and a service?

A facility is a place which has been specially provided for a particular activity to take place or for a particular need to be met, e.g. a restaurant or public toilets.

A service is an activity provided to meet someone else's needs, e.g. home delivery pizzas or powered transport around airports for people with mobility problems.

Tourist destinations and attractions often list services and facilities together.

For example Table 1.7 shows the list of things available for visitors at Fountains Abbey, a National Trust property.

For disabled visitors ...	For families ...	For education groups ...
Minibus to Abbey	Baby rooms	Resource book for teachers
Powered runarounds and wheelchairs	High chairs and children's menu	Education Officer
Adapted WC available	Activities programme	
Level access to Abbey grounds and visitor centre		
Guided tours for visually impaired people		

Table 1.7

Exercise 1.14

1 Discuss which of the things listed in Table 1.7 you think is a service and which is a facility.

2 Fountains Abbey was built in 1132 and is the largest monastic ruin in Britain. Nearby is both a mediaeval deer park and an eighteenth century landscaped water garden. List some other facilities and services you would expect to find at a large historic site such as this.

Here are some other facilities and services often found in tourist destinations:

✪ **Amusement arcades**

✪ **Bus services between hotels and the beach**

✪ **Car hire services**

✪ **Cinemas**

✪ **Coach and car parks**

✪ **Currency exchange offices**

✪ **Qualified guides**

✪ **Signposted walks and scenic drives**

✪ **Tourist Information Centres**

✪ **Post Offices**

✪ **Taxi services**

✪ **Theatres**

Information is a very important service which tourists need. It helps them to find places of interest. In the UK this information can be found in Tourist Information Centres which provide guides, maps, books, accommodation details and transport timetables.

Activity 1.11

1 You are going to a destination for the first time. Make a list of all the questions you would want to ask. You could choose examples like Australia, Jamaica or Mexico.

continued

continued

2   Write down the different methods you could use to find out the information needed to answer your questions. Say which would be the best methods and why.

3   Choose a destination in your area and collect some information about facilities and services provided there. Suggest some suitable activities for each of the following groups staying in the region:

A party of 20 foreign students on a school exchange

An elderly couple fond of walking, music and dining out

A family of 5 with children aged 4, 9 and 13

A touring netball or cricket team

Who provides facilities and services for tourists?

Industrial activity is often divided into three sectors:

✪ **The public sector**

✪ **The private sector**

✪ **The voluntary sector**

The main differences between the three sectors are:

Public sector

Organisations and facilities, often providing a public service, funded mainly by central or local government through national or local taxation, by means of grants or in the form of subsidies.

Private sector

Companies providing products and services in order to generate financial profit.

Voluntary sector

Generally non-profit making organisations and facilities dependent on volunteers, and often serving special needs and interest groups.

The role of these sectors in the leisure and tourism industries

Many facilities provided for tourists belong to the private sector. This includes businesses like travel agents, hotels and tourist attractions which make a profit by selling products to the public.

The public sector also plays a part in the tourism industry. National and regional tourist boards get some of their income from public funds. They are responsible for providing tourist information and in some areas carry out tasks like inspecting hotels. Local authorities often appoint tourism officers to encourage the development of local tourism.

The voluntary sector also plays a part in tourism. Tourist attractions like restored steam railways and old country houses are often staffed by volunteers. These people are not paid for the work they do.

Many new tourism developments are the result of partnerships between the private and public sectors.

Organisations like the National Trust, which relies on voluntary staff, also makes money from commercial activities such as shops selling souvenirs.

Steam engine restorer – voluntary sector

A National Trust shop NTPL. Photographer – Chris King

The two tables below show some examples of leisure and tourism facilities which are provided by either the public, private or voluntary sectors.

Sector	Interests within sector	Examples of leisure provision
Public sector	Central government	Royal Parks, National Sports Centres, e.g. Lilleshall, Bisham Abbey
	Local government	playing fields, swimming pools, leisure centres, parks, gardens, allotments, community centres, libraries, regional theatres
Private sector	Members' only sports clubs	golf, squash, snooker, health and fitness centres, country clubs
	Payment on admission entertainment centres	cinemas, theatres, bowling alleys, skating rinks, dance halls, professional sport, theme parks, bingo halls
	Employee benefits	company-owned sports grounds, bars, dance and entertainment venues
Voluntary sector	Amateur sports clubs and arts groups	amateur drama/opera groups, hockey, rugby, cricket and soccer clubs
	Interest groups and charities	conservation and heritage groups, community action groups, youth organisations

Sector	Interests within sector	Examples of tourism provision
Public sector	Central government	English Tourist Board, British Tourist Authority
	Local government	tourism information signs, regional tourism strategies
Private sector	transport companies	airlines, ferry and rail operators, coach companies, car hire firms
	payment on admission attractions	theme parks, museums, zoos, country houses
	travel service providers	travel agents, tour operators, currency and travel insurance services
	catering and accommodation providers	hotel chains, caravan sites, motorway service stations, restaurants
Voluntary sector	interest groups	heritage societies, conservation groups
	charities	supporting special needs, e.g. Holiday Care Service, some small tourist attractions, e.g. Bekonscot Model Village, staffing properties open to the public, e.g. National Trust

Activity
1.12

Find one example each of a business or organisation which you think belongs in the public, private and voluntary sectors. Briefly describe its main activities.

Business/organisation	Sector	Main activities
	public	
	private	
	voluntary	

For each of the three businesses/organisations you have found, suggest an activity they might try in partnership with a business/organisation from another sector. For example a tourist attraction might host an open air concert in support of a charitable organisation arranging days out for young people with disabilities.

What would be the benefits of these activities in each case to the two partner businesses or organisations?

Planning a holiday

2

What will the weather be like?

Will it be warm enough?

Chapter 3 looks at the different kinds of destination you can choose to stay in. This chapter looks at some of the decisions and plans you have to make in order to decide whether a particular destination will be suitable.

Figure 2.1 Climate is very important

Climate is important for many people going on holiday. They want sunshine if they have chosen a beach holiday. They want some snow if they have gone skiing. Sailing and windsurfing need some wind.

The weather affects the time of year people go on holiday. They don't want to spend all their time sheltering from heavy rain or finding it too hot to do anything at all. People often choose destinations where the weather is predictable – in other words where it is nearly always the same at a particular time of year.

This is one of Britain's problems as a tourist destination. It quite often rains in the summer months, when it is warmest.

Activity 2.1

Use climate information in holiday brochures to help you to fill in the following table:

Destination	The best month to visit would be ...	Because ...
Florida		
Scotland		
Hong Kong		
Switzerland		
New Zealand		

For each of these destinations try to work out which would be the worst months, from the point of view of climate, to visit them and explain why.

Not all holiday-makers like hot weather. Consider the following examples:

✪ **People who have come from a very hot climate**

✪ **People on an activity holiday, e.g. improving your tennis skills**

✪ **People with very fair skin**

They may all want to stay in a destination which is warm but not too hot.

The main factors affecting temperature

How hot a destination is depends on where it is and the type of landscape which surrounds it. Table 2.1 shows the things which affect temperature most.

Latitude	In general temperatures become cooler as you move from the Equator towards the North and South Poles
Altitude	Usually the higher above sea level you are, the cooler the temperature becomes
Ocean currents	These can be warm or cold. Winds blowing from the sea to the land can raise or lower land temperatures
Distance from the sea	Differences in temperature between land and sea and the effects of winds can mean that coastal areas are sometimes warmer or colder than inland areas
Winds	These can be warm or cold and so can have the effect of raising or lowering temperatures
Cloud cover and humidity	Heavy cloud cover can reduce differences in day and night time temperatures. Areas without cloud cover often have high daytime temperatures, but are much colder at night. Humid air also retains heat more than dry air so that places where the air is very humid, like the tropics, often stay very warm at night
Aspect	Aspect is more likely to affect climate the further away you are from the Equator. This is because in the tropics the sun is always high in the sky and so all slopes are exposed to it. Further away from the equator south-facing slopes will be warmer in the Northern Hemisphere while north-facing slopes will be warmer in the Southern Hemisphere

Table 2.1

Activity 2.2

Show the information in Table **2.1** in a poster suitable for display in your Travel and Tourism classroom.

Effects of temperature on tourists

Temperature may affect tourists in a number of ways. Areas which are hot and humid, like the tropics, make any activity seem much harder, as well as increasing the risk of heat stroke. Hot, dry climates are popular with tourists wishing to acquire a suntan, though increasingly the dangers of exposure to direct sunlight are being publicised. Without precautions, sunburn and dehydration are serious risks in these conditions. Breezes may be helpful in cooling the skin temperature though they will not reduce the potentially harmful effect of the sun's rays.

Other weather factors affecting tourists

Rain can affect tourists. Many of the things they may want to do take place in the open air, so destinations with low rainfall are usually popular. Some places with high annual rainfall still attract tourists because the rain only falls in certain seasons of the year or because it comes in very short heavy showers.

Winds can make it feel much colder. The wind chill factor may make conditions for tourists less pleasant than a day with similar temperatures but no wind.

Exercise 2.1

Bridgetown is the capital of the Caribbean island of Barbados. This island is the most easterly of the West Indian group of islands known as the Windward Islands. Trade winds give the island a mild, subtropical climate.

Study the data in the graphs below which provide a year round picture of Bridgetown's climate.

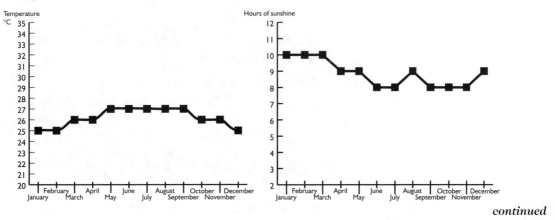

continued

continued

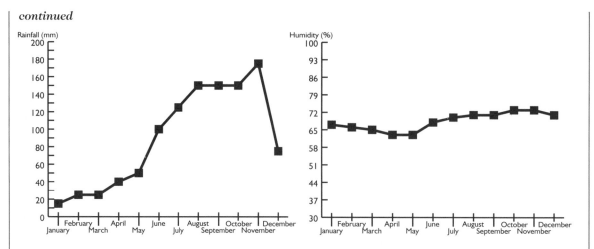

Rainfall (mm) — Humidity (%)

1 Which do you think would be the three ***most*** popular months for tourists? Why is this?

2 Which do you think would be the three ***least*** popular months for tourists? Why is this?

3 Which do you think are the months in which the majority of tourists from Europe are most likely to take holidays?

4 Does this cause any problems for people in Barbados who want to attract more tourists from Europe?

5 What could they do about these problems?

Snow also affects tourists who want to go skiing. Most ski resorts are at altitude, partly because you need slopes to ski but also because this brings more likelihood of snow.

Ski resorts have to be at high altitude to ensure a high chance of snow

Most ski resorts are above the snow line for only the winter months, but this means they often attract visitors at times of year when traditional summer resorts are least popular. Skiing can only take place when visibility is good and so the best climate for skiing is plenty of sunshine, little wind, and at least 3 or 4 months when visitors can expect a good covering of snow.

In the European Alps there is generally snow from November to April, though its depth and suitability for skiing may vary from resort to resort. The snow is often accompanied by dry, cold weather conditions which mean that, though the temperature is cold, skiers can enjoy bright sunlight.

Exercise 2.2

A suitable climate for skiing depends on four main factors:

★   Temperature

★   Wind speed

★   Precipitation (snow)

★   Visibility

Complete the sentences below to explain why each of these factors is important for skiing:

High temperatures are not good for skiing because _____

_____.

Strong winds are not good for skiing because _____

_____.

Very heavy snow or very light snow may not be good for skiing because_____

_____.

Fog or heavy snowstorms are not good for skiing because_____

_____.

Use pictures from ski brochures to help you to write a short report explaining how ski equipment helps tourists to be safe and to enjoy the sport.

How far is it?

More people who live in London go on holiday to Cornwall than to the Isle of Arran. There are a number of possible reasons for this, including:

- ✪ **Cornwall is nearer and takes less time to reach**

- ✪ **The transport links to the Isle of Arran are not as good as those to Cornwall**

For some people a long journey may put them off choosing certain destinations. This may be because:

they dislike flying or travelling by sea;

they have young children who may be hard to entertain;

they get uncomfortable on long journeys.

Long journeys can be difficult for some people

However, some tourists don't mind a long and difficult journey because they are looking for destinations which not many other people visit. Remoteness can be an advantage to a destination which wishes to concentrate on a luxury market and exclude mass tourism.

The following example highlights two factors affecting choice of destination.

distance	*how far the destination is from the places containing people who can afford to go there*
transport links	*whether the transport available and where the destination is situated make the destination easy or difficult to get to*

Distance related to cost

In order to become a tourist you have to want to travel. You also need enough money to get you to your destination and to pay for accommodation. You must also be able to afford to take time off work. This means that the majority of tourists to other countries come from the richer countries of the world, for example the United States, Britain, Germany and Japan. There are not so many international travellers from countries where people earn less money.

Activity 2.3

Use an atlas to help you make some suggestions about the most popular foreign destinations for people living in the countries shown below:

Country where people live	Foreign destinations they could visit easily
Holland	
USA	
New Zealand	
Malaysia	
Morocco	
Austria	

Tourist destinations

Think about the disadvantages of long journeys:

- ❂ **They are more tiring**
- ❂ **They take more time**
- ❂ **They usually cost more**
- ❂ **They may require changes from one transport system to another**

✪ **Visa and health requirements may be more complicated**

✪ **The cultural differences may be greater than would be found in destinations nearer home**

We have already seen that most international tourists come from richer countries. This means that tourist destinations often develop within a reasonably short journey time from these countries. Many of the most popular summer holiday destinations in Europe are in the Mediterranean. There are destinations for winter sports in the Alps and Pyrenees. Most of these resorts are only 2 or 3 hours' flying time away from their main markets.

Figure 2.1 shows some of the main directions in which tourists travel. It shows the areas where most tourists come from and the areas which most of them travel to.

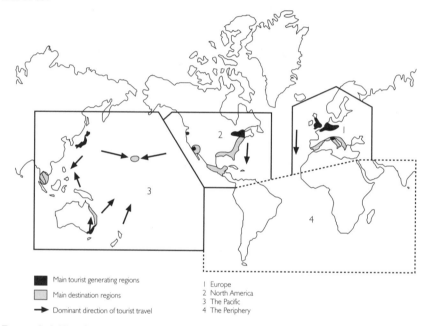

■ Main tourist generating regions

▢ Main destination regions

➤ Dominant direction of tourist travel

1 Europe
2 North America
3 The Pacific
4 The Periphery

Figure 2.1 The four main tourist regions of the world

Time differences

Something else which puts some people off travelling long distances is having to cross different time zones. Figure 2.2 shows how places a long way away have different times.

People travelling eastwards or westwards often find that they experience 'jet lag' after a long flight. It is hard to get used to the different time and they find they can't sleep at night. This feeling usually only lasts a day or two. Travelling north or south, for example from England to South Africa, doesn't have the same effect because the times in the place you leave and the place you arrive at are almost the same.

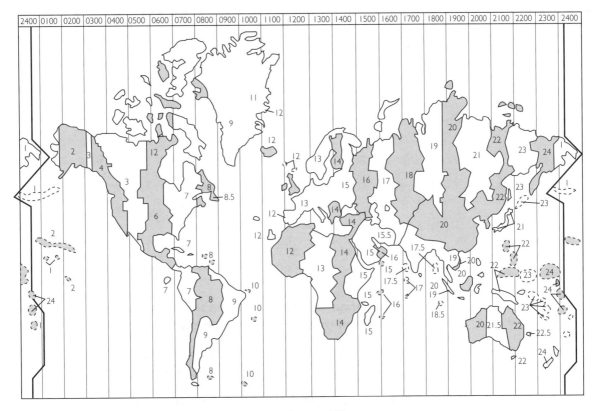

Figure 2.2 International time differences

Exercise 2.3

1 Use the time zone map in Figure 2.2 and an atlas to complete the following table:

If it is ...	What time is it in ...
9.30 a.m. in London	Sydney?
6.15 p.m. in New York	Moscow?
11.20 a.m. in Tokyo	Los Angeles?
1 p.m. in Capetown	Madrid?

2 Your flight leaves London at 8 a.m. and takes 8 hours to fly to Delhi.

   What time will it be in Delhi when your plane lands?

3 Your flight leaves London at 4 p.m. and takes 7 hours to fly to New York.

   What time will it be in New York when your plane lands?

Transport links

Transport services to tourist destinations affect their popularity. A mountainous Greek island which can only be reached by a 16-hour ferry journey from the mainland is unlikely to attract as many tourists as an island with an airport which can handle international and domestic flights.

There are more airline flights in Western Europe, the Eastern United States and East Asia than in most other parts of the world. These regular services allow a big exchange of tourists between these areas.

Not all transport services can carry large numbers of passengers. There may be a number of reasons for this:

- ✪ **Physical circumstances, such as a short runway at an airport or a shortage of public transport vehicles**

- ✪ **Low demand, which means that the companies providing the transport links only run occasional services**

- ✪ **Government control of the numbers to protect the environment and the overall appearance of the destination**

Many tourists do not like their destinations to be too crowded. There is a limit to the number of people a destination can cope with. Two things help to set a limit on the number of visitors:

- ✪ **The number of rooms available for them to stay in**

- ✪ **How many people the available transport links can carry to and from the destination**

Exercise 2.4

Study the chart below which indicates the average distance travelled by people taking short break holidays in the United Kingdom.

1   What conclusions would you draw from this information?

2   How might your Regional Tourist Board use the information in its attempts to attract more visitors to your region?

continued

continued

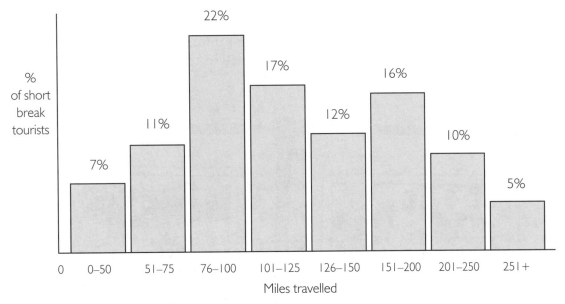

Miles travelled by short break tourists

3 Use the information in the chart to draw up a list of the main areas you would expect most people taking a short break in your area to have travelled from.

Maps, bus and railway timetables, and mileage charts would be useful in providing evidence on which to base your conclusions.

4 Show the conclusions you came to in task **3** in a diagram or graph.

How much will it cost?

The cost of your holiday will depend on a number of things:

- ✪ **Where you go**
- ✪ **Where you depart from**
- ✪ **How long you stay**
- ✪ **What sort of accommodation you choose**
- ✪ **What means of transport you prefer**
- ✪ **What time of year you travel**
- ✪ **How many people there are travelling with you**

Discuss which of the following holidays you think would cost a lot and which ones would be medium priced and which ones would be cheap.

Types of holiday

continued

continued

This holiday would be ...	Cheap	Medium	Expensive
A family of six on a week's canal cruising in France			
A couple on honeymoon at an all inclusive resort in the Caribbean			
Two students on a week's camping holiday in Devon			
Two friends on a week's fishing trip in Ireland			
A widow on a coach tour of Italy			
A couple on a three-week cruise to see the animals on the Galapagos Islands			

Tick one of the columns in each case.

Now look at holiday brochures and newspaper advertisements.

List the three most expensive and the three least expensive holidays you can find.

What do your lists tell you about what makes a holiday expensive or cheap?

Activity 2.5

1 Work out the total cost of the following holiday:

Three friends plan to spend 14 days on the Greek island of Zakynthos in June. They wish to fly from Manchester. They have chosen the Amalia Beach apartments. While they are on the island they want to hire a Class A car for the 2 weeks of their stay.

Prices in the table below include flights and accommodation. They do not include insurance, flight supplements and car hire.

Amalia Beach apartments – prices per person

	1–25 May	26 May–1 July	2 July–31 August	1 Sept–31 Oct
7 nights	£270	£320	£390	£295
14 nights	£295	£375	£490	£325

Beach & Son Ltd – holiday insurance cover per person

no of days holiday	0–7 days	8–15 days	15–23 days
premium	£29	£44	£59

continued

continued

Flight supplements – per person

airport	Luton	Stansted	Manchester	Birmingham
supplement	£12	£18	£24	£22

Car hire

	one week	two weeks	three weeks
Class A	£55	£100	£140
Class B	£70	£130	£185
Class C	£85	£160	£230

2 How much would it have cost them to go for 1 week only?

3 How much more would it have cost them to have the same holiday in August?

4 Act out a role play in which the travel agent explains and answers questions about how the price of the holiday described in task 1 has been worked out.

How tour operators set the price of a holiday

The difficulties of setting a price for a holiday

Tour operators have to work out how much to charge for the holidays they put together. This is not easy because:

✪ **People often book holidays many months before they are due to go**

✪ **This means the price has to be fixed long before the holiday takes place**

✪ **The costs of the holiday for the tour operator can go up during this time because of things like rises in fuel prices**

Holiday bargains

✪ **Changes in currency exchange rates can also mean that the tour operator has to pay more for things like overseas airline facilities than they had planned for**

✪ **Changes in currency exchange rates can also make destinations suddenly seem more expensive so that it becomes difficult to sell holidays to them at the original price**

✪ **Tour operators may feel they have to cut the original price of the holiday if other companies are selling similar tours more cheaply**

Calculating the price of a package holiday

The price of a holiday package has to include:

payment to accommodation owners;

payment to transport providers;

commission to the agents selling the holiday (unless it is sold direct);

profit for the tour operator.

Look at the example below:

Hava Niceday Holidays –
breakdown of cost of 2-week villa holiday in Florida

Accommodation: Villa Verde Apartments 2 weeks
@ £59 per week = £118

Flights: return charter flight Gatwick–Orlando = £399

Coach transfers: Orlando–Fort Lauderdale = £ 38
return

TOTAL: **£555**

+ travel agent's commission (10%): £ 55

+ operator's profit: £ 75

TOTAL COST OF HOLIDAY £685

Table 2.2 gives some more details about each of the elements of the cost of a package holiday:

payment to accommodation owners	Bigger tour operators, booking hundreds of rooms in the same destination will be able to get cheaper rates from the owners
payment to transport providers	Tour operators often use charter flights to holiday destinations. These flights are usually arranged at times of year when many people want to travel. Being sure of filling all the seats on the plane helps to lower the cost of the tickets
commission to travel agents	Tour operators pay travel agents a commission in return for selling their holidays to the public. Often the more holidays an agent sells, the higher the rate of commission they receive
advertising and promotion	The tour operator has to pay for brochures to advertise their holidays. They would have to think about this and other business costs in working out what profit they expect to make
profit for the tour operator	Profit is usually worked out by adding a lump sum to the overall cost of the holiday package. This sum will vary according to the destination involved

Table 2.2

1 Compare the brochure prices for a 2-week holiday for a family of four to *three* different destinations.

List what you think are the reasons for the differences in prices of holidays to these three destinations.

2 Choose a tourist destination in the UK which you think people from your area might go to for a holiday.

List three different ways of travelling to it and three different types of accommodation available there.

Do some research to find out the different prices which you would have to pay for different methods of transport to and accommodation in this destination.

Booking a holiday

Once you have decided on a particular holiday, there are three main ways of booking it:

Payment details have to be sorted out

✪ **Getting a travel agent to do it for you**

✪ **Filling in and sending off the booking form in the holiday brochure**

✪ **Ringing up the tour operator and booking direct**

Whichever way you make a booking you will have to provide full details about the holiday you want to book and the people who will be on holiday with you. You will also have to buy some travel insurance, unless you have this already.

Payment details will have to be sorted out, including whether you want to pay by cash, cheque or credit card. You will have to pay a deposit when you make the booking. If the departure date is very close you may have to pay the whole price of the holiday when making your booking. Otherwise you will probably have to pay a deposit now and the rest about 10 weeks before you are due to go.

Exercise 2.5

Complete the booking form below for yourself and three other people, either members of your family or friends, who will be taking the holiday together.

HOLIDAY REQUIRED   AWDAY OLIDAYS BOOKING FORM

Resort	Hotel	Departure date	No. of nights

DETAILS OF PASSENGERS TRAVELLING

Title	First name (in capitals)	Surname (in capitals)	Age (if under 16)

DEPARTURE AIRPORT (please tick your requirement)

Luton ☐	Gatwick ☐	Birmingham ☐	Manchester ☐

CAR HIRE (please tick your requirements)

Please reserve a group   A ☐   B ☐   C ☐   D ☐   car for me

from.................................to ....for.........................days

Pick up airport ☐	hotel ☐	Drop off airport ☐	hotel ☐

SPECIAL REQUESTS   Please use this space to detail any special requirements such as adjoining rooms, vegetarian meals on flights etc.

PAYMENT DETAILS

Deposit of £40 per passenger of full amount if travel is within 10 weeks	£..........................
Insurance premium	£..........................
Enclosed cheque/postal order	£..........................

I have read and understand the booking conditions relating to the above holiday and I accept them on my own behalf and on behalf of all other persons named on this booking form.

Signature.. Date.............................

PAYMENT BY CREDIT CARD

I wish to pay by ACCESS/BARCLAYCARD*
please charge the deposit*/full amount* to my card account (*please indicate as applicable)

CREDIT CARD NUMBER   ☐ ☐ ☐ ☐ ☐ ☐ ☐ ☐ ☐ ☐ ☐ ☐ ☐ ☐

Expiry date of card.. Signature...

Address.. (Postcode) ....

Choosing where to go

3

Seaside resorts

The first thing many people think of when the idea of a holiday comes up is sun and sand. Holidays by the sea have been popular for a long time. They offer the chance for people to relax. Here are some things people say about seaside holidays:

> 'The children love playing on the beach, building sandcastles, paddling in the sea, donkey rides and exploring rock pools . . .'

> 'There's such a lot to do at a good seaside resort, things like funfairs, amusement arcades, and summer shows . . .'

> 'I just like sitting watching and listening to the waves. Sometimes I'll read; sometimes I just watch the world go by. It's very relaxing . . .'

> 'Where else can you try things like windsurfing and canoeing in the daytime and check out the clubs and discos at night?'

These comments suggest that seaside resorts appeal to people of different ages and interests. They also suggest that not all seaside resorts are the same. Some are small and quiet; others are larger with enough facilities for large numbers of visitors.

Wind-surfing at the seaside

Activity 3.1

Use an atlas to find out where in the UK the places in the table below are. You will need to look in the index for the place names and then use the page and grid references to find out if they are on the coast or not.

Tick those which are seaside resorts.

Weston-super-Mare		Ulverston	
Lewes		Mablethorpe	
Ormskirk		Devizes	
Broadstairs		Prestatyn	
Southport		Walton-on-the-Naze	
Beverley		North Walsham	
Carmarthen		Swanage	
Filey		Brixham	
Tenby		Honiton	
Liskeard		Louth	

The early growth of British seaside resorts

People started to go to the seaside in large numbers towards the end of the last century. There were a number of reasons for this:

Sea bathing was thought to be good for your health

- ✪ **They wanted to get away from the industrial cities with their polluted air**

- ✪ **They were earning more money as a result of industrial growth**

- ✪ **They had time off on Bank Holidays for the first time**

- ✪ **Ferry and rail services between industrial towns and coastal resorts were increasing**

- ✪ **Sea bathing was thought by many people to be good for your health**

Resorts like Brighton and Southport grew very quickly because they could be reached easily by rail from cities like London and Manchester.

The way seaside resorts developed

One thing . . .	Often led to another . . .
a railway link was set up	a hotel was built close to the station
the sea and the beach were the main attractions	accommodation was built along the sea front
the sea was too cold for some who wanted exercise	piers, gardens and promenades were built to provide attractive settings for walking
more people owned private cars	coastal roads became busier and the pressure for parking spaces increased
more people wanted rooms with sea views	sea-front hotels grew taller and land prices by the sea increased

Activity 3.2

1 Collect six postcards featuring photographs of seaside resorts.

2 List the similarities and differences which the pictures on the cards suggest about the different resorts.

3 Choose one postcard which does not have any writing about the seaside resort on it. If someone was planning to use it as a poster to attract people to the resort, what words might they add to try and get people to come?

Exercise 3.1

What does this figure show about the way a traditional seaside resort might have developed? You could refer to a resort you know in order to help your explanation.

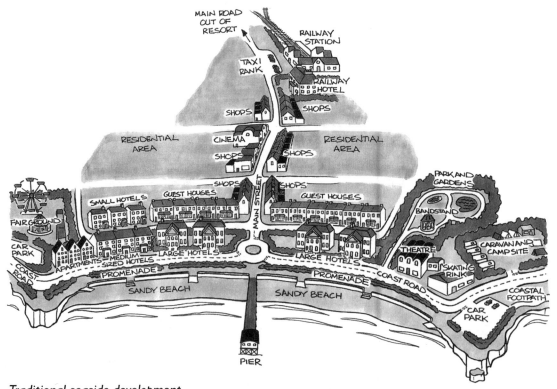

Traditional seaside development

Decline of traditional British seaside resorts

The popularity of the British seaside resorts began to fall in the 1960s. There were several main reasons for this, all of them linked:

✪ **The growth of cheap Mediterranean package holidays**

✪ **The unpredictable English weather and better chances of sunny weather in warmer climates**

✪ **Advertising suggesting foreign holidays offered a more exciting experience**

✪ **Television programmes increasing awareness of other destinations**

As more people took their holidays overseas, the number of people visiting British seaside resorts began to fall. Many who did visit stayed only a day or two rather than the traditional 2 weeks in the summer, causing many hotels and boarding houses to close or else to change their function to hostels or retirement homes.

Fewer visitors meant less money was spent in the resorts and there were fewer tourism jobs available. This loss of income also meant there was less money to spend on keeping buildings and facilities well decorated and in good repair.

Restoration and promotion of seaside resorts

In more recent times British seaside resorts have tried to find ways to improve their appearance and to win back visitors. Some of the things they have done are:

✪ **Restoring buildings to their original appearance**

✪ **Landscaping, especially along the sea front**

✪ **Using advertising to persuade people to come and see traditional seaside architecture such as stations, hotels, piers and civic buildings**

✪ **Using joint promotions with rail and coach companies to encourage people to take out of season weekend and short breaks at the seaside**

✪ **Developing indoor facilities which don't depend on good weather**

Landscaping on Tyneside

Exercise 3.2

A group of students is due to visit a seaside resort. One of their tasks is to write a report about the condition of some of the facilities provided for tourists. They have been told that they should observe each of the following things in the resort:

★ *Information signs*

★ *The appearance of shop fronts*

★ *Parking spaces*

★ *Parks and gardens*

★ *Entertainments*

Draw up a list of questions for each of the five areas above. Your questions should tell the students what sorts of things to look for, so that they collect good evidence for their report. To help you get started, one example for each area is given below:

continued

continued

Area to look at ...	Question to ask yourself ...
information signs	Are these placed where they can be easily read by anyone?
the appearance of shop fronts	Does their appearance match the upper part of the buildings in which they are?
parking spaces	How much are visitors charged to park their cars near the town centre?
parks and gardens children?	Do parks and gardens have playing facilities for young
entertainments	What are the opening hours of the main entertainments for tourists?

The countryside

Some people prefer holidays in the countryside. The countryside is popular because it can offer holidaymakers the chance to enjoy:

✪ **Attractive landscape**

✪ **Peace and quiet**

✪ **Activities such as walking, climbing, boating and observing wildlife**

Visits to the countryside became much more popular as the number of people owning cars grew. Country roads and villages were not built to cope with heavy traffic. Councils in popular rural areas, such as parts of the Lake District, have to plan ways of making sure that large numbers of visitors do not spoil the countryside they have come to see.

National Parks

More visitors to the countryside means more chance of damage. This includes things like:

✪ **Footpath erosion**

✪ **Destruction of wildlife habitats**

Walking in the countryside

- ✪ **Damage to crops**

- ✪ **Tourism facilities which spoil previously attractive views**

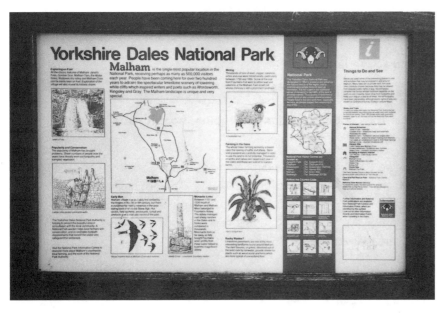

National Park sign

Other problems, such as an increase in litter and noise, can also occur in towns and cities which receive a lot of visitors.

One way of trying to deal with these problems is to create National Parks. There are now ten National Parks in England and Wales, covering these areas:

Brecon Beacons
Dartmoor
Exmoor
Lake Distrct

Northumberland
North Yorkshire Moors
Peak District

Pembrokeshire Coast
Snowdonia
Yorkshire Dales

Other areas, like the Broads and the New Forest, do not have the title of National Park, but have been given some protection against developments which are thought to be unsuitable.

Exercise 3.3

The map below shows an outline of where each of the ten National Parks, and the two other special areas – the Broads and the New Forest – can be found. Each one is marked with a number.

Use an atlas or a road map to help you complete the following table:

1		7	
2		8	
3		9	
4		10	
5		11	
6		12	

National Parks in England and Wales

When the idea of National Parks was first suggested in Britain, there were three main aims:

○ **To protect these areas from damage and unsuitable developments**

○ **To allow walkers to explore them without barriers**

○ **To protect the plants and animals found in them**

The National Parks in Britain were set up in 1949. The people with the job of managing them had two main responsibilities:

○ **To preserve and improve the natural beauty of the Parks**

○ **To encourage the general public to enjoy visiting the Parks**

Exercise 3.4

Discuss which of the following ideas would encourage an increase in visitors to a National Park:

1 Introducing a *Park and Ride* scheme from different places at the edge of the Park

2 Advertising the attractions of a day in the country on local radio

3 Banning camping except on three official camp sites

4 Holding a stage of a car rally on forest trails within the Park

5 Banning the playing of transistor radios in all picnic areas

6 Placing advertisements on railway stations in the nearest towns outside the Park

7 Building a Tourist Information Centre in the Park

8 Putting signposts on the nearest motorway routes

9 Making a TV documentary about the lives of people who live within the Park

10 Building a new main road round the edge of the Park

Which of these ideas might have a harmful effect on the Park?

Looking after the countryside

The countryside is not just for the use of visitors. Other important activities take place there, such as:

farming

military exercises

forestry

quarrying

scientific research

people living

The people who carry out these activities and those who live there may not want visitors. For example, many farmers think visitors will damage crops or worry livestock.

Some things can be done to stop this.

✪ **Careful signposting of walks and bridleways helps to keep people off farm land**

✪ **Rebuilding of walls and stiles keeps people on official footpaths**

✪ **Using weights to make sure that gates close on their own stops livestock straying**

Making the countryside accessible while safeguarding the interests of those who live and work there

Brochures and newspapers advertising the attractions of the countryside often include the Country Code (Table 3.1).

The Country Code

- Enjoy the countryside and respect its life and work
- Guard against all risk of fire
- Fasten all gates
- Keep your dogs under close control
- Keep to public paths across farm land
- Use gates and stiles to cross fences, hedges and walls

- Leave livestock, crops and machinery alone
- Take your litter home
- Help to keep all water clean
- Protect wildlife, plants and trees
- Take special care on country roads
- Make no unnecessary noise

Table 3.1

Activity 3.3

Read the following information about country parks:

Country parks are much smaller than National Parks. They have usually been specially developed so that people who live in towns and cities can reach them easily. They allow people who live in urban areas to experience the feeling of being in the country without having to travel a long way to get there.

Country parks usually have a number of facilities for visitors, including:

car parks   *tea rooms*
toilets   *playgrounds*

Country parks may attract people who would otherwise have travelled into the countryside. This could help to reduce the crowds and traffic in the more popular country areas.

Most of the people who visit country parks are on day trips.

1   Choose a site near the town or city where you live (or the nearest one to your home) which you think could be developed into a country park.

2   Draw a sketch map of the existing site and mark on it suitable locations for the facilities which you think would be necessary to make it popular in your area. Explain why you have chosen to site these facilities in the places you have.

3   Show on your sketch map the directions from which you think the majority of visitors would approach the new country park and explain how this would affect:

    a local residents;

    b the company awarded the contract to design the new park;

    c the company awarded the contract to manage the new park.

Some important organisations

Three organisations whose work affects the countryside are:

The Countryside Commission

✪ **Receives funds from the government**

✪ **Gives grants to help conservation projects**

✪ **Gives the government advice about the countryside**

✪ **Helps to protect public rights of way**

The Forestry Commission

✪ **Manages woods and forests**

✪ **Plants new trees**

✪ **Gives advice on planting trees**

✪ **Sells timber to businesses**

✪ **Provides visitor facilities such as marked trails and picnic areas**

The National Trust

✪ **Manages countryside properties, including country houses and gardens**

✪ **Educates people about conservation and restoration**

✪ **Looks after important landscape areas such as coastline and heaths**

Three organisations whose work affects the countryside

Exercise 3.5

Discuss which of these points of view you agree with and which ones you disagree with:

'People who want to visit the countryside should pay something towards the cost of keeping it looking nice.'

'Farmers and landowners should be able to keep people off their land so that they can't do any damage.'

'The countryside belongs to everyone.'

Towns and cities

People come in to towns and cities for different reasons. Some of these reasons change over time.

Here are some examples.

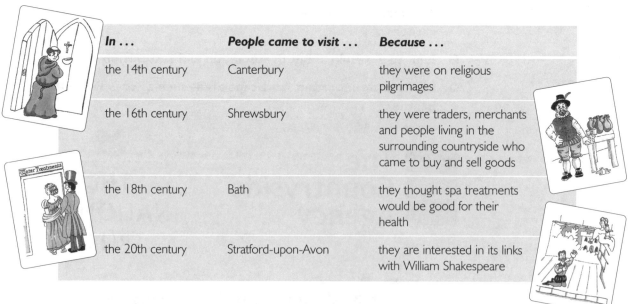

In ...	People came to visit ...	Because ...
the 14th century	Canterbury	they were on religious pilgrimages
the 16th century	Shrewsbury	they were traders, merchants and people living in the surrounding countryside who came to buy and sell goods
the 18th century	Bath	they thought spa treatments would be good for their health
the 20th century	Stratford-upon-Avon	they are interested in its links with William Shakespeare

People go to towns for different reasons

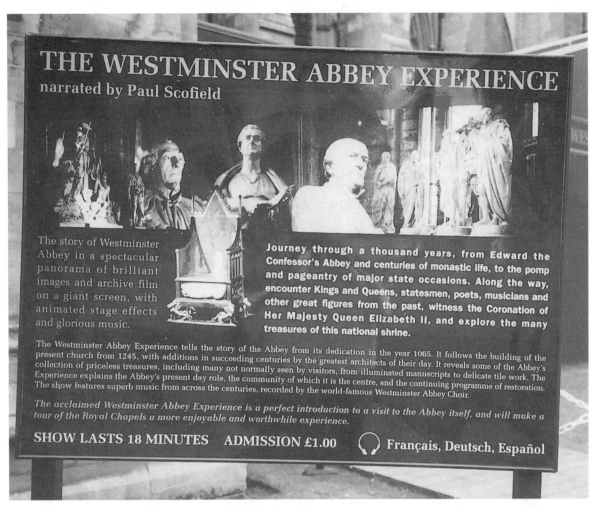

Visiting an old building

Nowadays people often visit towns or cities to look at old buildings. They might want to see:

A cathedral (e.g. in Canterbury or Liverpool)

A castle (e.g. in Warwick or Caernarvon)

Roman remains (e.g. in St Albans or Bath)

A college (e.g. in Dublin or Oxford)

Old houses (e.g. in Chester or Bath)

These buildings are often in the centre of older towns and cities. Some of them are interesting because of their design. They are thought to be the best examples of the work of past and present architects.

Others are interesting because they help visitors to get an idea of what life in the past was like.

Activity 3.4

1   Collect some information about the things in a town or city near to where you live which most visitors like to see.

Here are some ways of collecting this information:

Ring up the Tourist Information Centre.

Borrow a book about the town or city from your school or public library.

Visit the town or city and make notes about what you see.

2   Choose five places in the town or city which you think would be very popular with visitors.

Now complete this table:

Name of place of interest	What there is to see there	Why people want to see it
1		
2		
3		
4		
5		

3   Match the places of interest in Column **A** to the historic towns or cities in Column **B**:

A	B
Trinity College	Bath
Ashmolean Museum	Brighton
The Pantiles	Oxford
The Pavilion	Dublin
The Pump Rooms	York
The Yorvik Centre	Tunbridge Wells

Length of visits

Many visitors to towns and cities are on day trips. Because they have travelled to and from home in the same day they do not need any overnight accommodation. This means that towns and cities which attract a lot of visitors may have two disadvantages:

They suffer from crowds and traffic congestion

They do not receive as much income from visitors as they would if these people were staying longer

However, in recent years tour operators and hotel chains have increased the number of weekend and short break offers available which has in turn increased hotel occupancy in many historic towns.

Exercise 3.6

The graph below shows how many people visited some of the churches and cathedrals in the UK in 1993.

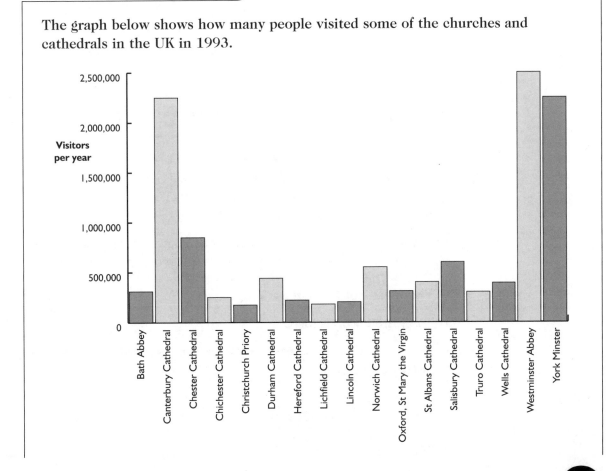

continued

1   Some of these visitor numbers are estimates. Why do you think some cathedrals and churches have to rely on estimates?

How can you tell that they are estimates?

Suggest a method which a church or cathedral could use to estimate its annual visitor numbers.

2   Which of the churches and cathedrals listed above do you think had some method of counting the actual number of visitors they received?

Suggest some methods they might have used to do this.

3   Which of these churches or cathedrals might you choose to visit for a day out if you were staying with relatives in each of the following places:

Great Yarmouth

Worcester

Falmouth

Margate

Bournemouth

(You will need to use a road atlas for this exercise, looking up the places in the index.)

Road traffic in historic towns

The streets in the centre of many historic towns were laid out hundreds of years ago. There was no motor traffic and the streets were often narrow and twisting. The centre is also usually where the most interesting old buildings are found.

Many visitors to historic towns come by car or by coach. This, along with the layout of the oldest streets, can create a number of problems:

- **There are not enough parking spaces**
- **Traffic pollution is increased**
- **No-one is allowed to alter buildings and roads which have historical interest**

Most historic towns have used different methods to try and solve these problems. Some of the ideas used are:

- **'Park and ride' schemes**

Car parking on the beach at Skegness

- ✪ **Short time limits on city centre parking**
- ✪ **Road signs directing motorists onto routes avoiding the town centre**
- ✪ **Pedestrian-only areas**

Building new roads does not always solve problems for historic cities. Sometimes new roads make it easier for people from further away to reach a town or city on a day trip. For example extending the M40 motorway means that many more people now live within a 2-hour drive of Oxford and Stratford-upon-Avon.

Exercise 3.7

Suggest a possible solution for each one of the following problems which tourism planners in a historic city are facing:

Problems ...	Solutions ...
Too many visitors to the Cathedral arrive mid morning	
The railway station is a long way from the city centre	
Only a small number of visitors are using the 'park and ride' scheme	
Streets in the centre of the town are very narrow	
A new shopping mall attracts a lot of cars because of its city centre multi-storey car park	

Preservation, conservation and restoration

Preservation, conservation and restoration are important in historic towns. These three words are slightly different in meaning.

Restoration of the Leaning Tower of Pisa

Preservation is trying to keep something looking like it does now.

Conservation is making sure that things last by protecting them from damage and decay.

Restoration is carrying out work to return something to the way it used to look in the past.

Appearance is very important in the centre of historic towns. Visitors like to get an impression of how buildings used to look. Sometimes the insides of these buildings have been converted so that they can be used as shops, banks or Tourist Information Centres.

It is important that the look of the outside of the buildings is not spoilt by brightly-coloured modern signs or advertisements.

Planning regulations in historic cities often stop the occupiers of older buildings from doing this.

Other features which attract visitors to towns

People do not visit towns just to see old buildings. Other features which they may want to see or experience include:

- ✪ **Shopping centres and markets**
- ✪ **Theatres and art galleries**
- ✪ **Museums**
- ✪ **Festivals, exhibitions and open air entertainments**
- ✪ **Parks and gardens**
- ✪ **Sports and leisure centres**

Activity 3.5

1   Look up the word 'heritage' in a dictionary and write down what it means.

2   List six things you might find in the centre of an old town which you think are linked to heritage.

3   Choose a local town and list six sites you think people interested in heritage might want to visit.

4   Prepare an itinerary for a heritage trail, including some guidance notes for visitors following it, which would give an interesting overall view of your chosen town's history.

New experiences

Holidays often give people a chance to try things they have never done before. Many people who enjoy activities like canoeing, pony trekking or skiing tried them for the first time when they were on holiday. Once they get interested in these activities they may choose their future holidays in places where these activities are provided.

Exercise 3.8

Divide the list of activities below into one of four groups:

Things I will never want to do

Things I have never done but would like to try

Things I have done but which didn't interest me

Things I have done and would like to try again

mountain climbing	mountain biking
pony trekking	fly fishing
taking lessons in Italian cookery	learning how to recognise antiques
taking a trip in a hot air balloon	taking dancing lessons
windsurfing	going bird-watching
taking a course on landscape painting	driving an off road vehicle
building a dry stone wall	orienteering
sailing	scuba diving

Something many people would like to try

Package holidays with a special interest focus

Not all the activities which people try on holiday are energetic. People can try things like learning oil painting techniques or how to renovate furniture. They can act as volunteers, helping to run private railway lines or repairing damage to footpaths, walls and canal banks.

Because more people have got bored with just sitting on a beach, tour operators and hotels have put together weekend breaks on which people can try out different activities.

New attractions at hotels!

One of the most popular of these short breaks is the murder mystery weekend. The plot of a detective story is acted out in the hotel, as the guests relax, mingle and dine. On the basis of their own observation and a variety of clues, guests have to try and solve the mystery.

One hotel on Dartmoor developed what they called `Full Moon Breaks'. These included midnight walks over the bleaker parts of the moor, late night readings of ghost stories and prizes for the guest who could describe the best nightmare!

Economic benefit of special interest holidays

The importance of activity holidays to centres like hotels, colleges and universities is that it enables them to earn revenue to cover their overheads at times when they are normally either little used or not in use at all. For example universities often run residential courses during the students' summer vacations while hotels offer activity breaks during autumn and winter, when they are less busy than in the summer months.

Activity 3.6

Plan a special interest weekend which could be offered by a hotel in the region in which you live.

You should include some information about:

why this type of weekend would be suitable in your area;

a schedule for the weekend, showing when and where activities would take place;

a list of the extra resources, staff and equipment which would be needed;

what sort of people you would aim to attract;

how you would advertise the break.

Present details about your weekend as a poster advertising it to potential customers.

Activity holidays and centres

Table 3.2 shows examples of some of the activities which people often try on holiday. It also shows the different kinds of centres which try to attract people interested in holidays based around these activities.

These activities do not always form part of a holiday. They only become activity holidays if accommodation, tuition and organised activities are all purchased as a package. This kind of holiday package can appeal to all types of consumer: independent adults; parents and families; school parties and children staying at summer camps.

Interest	Activity centre	Types of activity
sports	outward bound/outdoor centre	canoeing, mountaineering, orienteering
	water sports centre	windsurfing, scuba diving, power boat racing, white water rafting
	country hotel	hunting, fishing, clay pigeon shooting
hobbies	private railway society	maintenance, ticket collection, food service
	archaeological site	taking part in a 'dig'
	nature reserve	bird-watching, photography
arts	residential holiday centre	sketching, painting, visiting exhibitions
	university summer school	writing workshops, poetry readings, theatre tours
crafts	country hotel	cookery demonstrations, cookery classes
	country house	learning antique restoration techniques
education	school/college	working towards a degree or advanced job qualification
	driving centre	learning to drive, rallying, using a skid pan
conservation	National Park/National Trust property	repairing footpaths, laying down steps, mending walls
	canal	clearing towpaths, repairing lock gates
	listed building	decorating, restoring brickwork
community service	old people's home	visiting, entertaining, acting as voluntary driver
	seaside resort	accompanying disadvantaged children or travellers with disabilities

Safety at activity centres

Activity holidays are often more risky than others. In some cases, such as mountaineering or hang gliding, they should not be tried without a proper course of instruction.

Many activity centres plan courses and holidays for school children. These centres have to be sure that they employ staff with the proper experience and qualifications. They need to have the right skills, a knowledge of first aid, and an ability to get on well with visitors of all ages. They also need a responsible attitude, so that they take their supervision duties very seriously.

Some of the risks met on activity holidays need simple precautions. For example, pony trekkers should always wear hard hats. Other dangers are less

Instructors at activity centres must take their duties very seriously

predictable. For instance the hot summers of 1990 and 1991 led to an increase of algae in many stretches of fresh water. Anyone indulging in water sports who swallowed any of this could have become very ill from the after-effects. Some risks can be reduced by sensible preparation. Regular exercising before going on a skiing holiday can lessen the chances of pulled muscles, or twisted joints. These are often caused by lack of fitness.

The Department for Education has published a document called 'Safety in Outdoor Pursuits' which recommends safety procedures for all activity centres. It covers issues like:

✪ **The ratio of leaders and instructors to students**

✪ **The training and qualifications expected of instructors**

✪ **The inspection of equipment**

Exercise 3.9

You have to organise a party of twenty 12-year-olds who are going on a cliff top walk.

Brainstorm a list of safety concerns you would have to think about.

Below is a list of ten rules which you might draw up for the party to follow. However, some of them would probably be more useful than others.

Discuss which *six* rules you think would be most likely to ensure the safety of your party.

1 Always walk in pairs, holding hands.

continued

continued

2 Do not go closer than ten metres to the cliff's edge, unless you are following a path protected on the seaward side by a good fence or wall.

3 Check that you are wearing sensible walking shoes, particularly avoiding high heels or flip flops.

4 Allow no talking at any time.

5 Make sure that two or more adults are supervising the group at all times.

6 Allow the quicker walkers to go ahead at their own pace.

7 Take a lightweight rucksack for sandwiches, drinks and emergency rations.

8 Do not leave the marked footpath, unless a section of it appears sufficiently damaged to be dangerous.

9 Take along a football for a bit of entertainment along the route.

10 Carry a detailed local map and a compass, and tell a responsible person of your intended route.

Cruises

One type of holiday which has increased in popularity is the cruise. Accommodation is provided on board a cruise ship and holiday-makers visit a number of different destinations during their holiday.

Cruises attract people because:

- ✪ **Accommodation, meals and entertainment are included in the price**

- ✪ **Fly–cruise package holidays offer flights to the port of departure, so saving a long sea journey from English ports**

- ✪ **A wide range of fitness and sports activities are available**

- ✪ **A number of different interesting places can be visited without having to change your accommodation**

- ✪ **Services like currency exchange and guided tours are provided**

- ✪ **Food, language and surroundings are familiar**

Reproduced by courtesy of P&O Cruises

Exercise 3.10

You work in a travel agency.

How might you try to sell a cruise holiday to each of these three customers:

Donna MacIntosh (aged 68)

> 'I've never been abroad before. Most of my holidays have been in Scotland but I fancy a change. Somewhere it doesn't rain so much. I'm a widow – my husband died last year – and I'm a bit worried about travelling on my own because I don't speak any foreign languages.'

Robin Banks (aged 30)

> 'I'm looking for a fun holiday. I went to Ibiza last year. That was a good laugh but we ran out of money about half way through the holiday. We had to live on bread and cheese for three days.'

Helen Back (aged 44)

> 'I quite like the idea of a cruise but I'm a terrible sailor. I feel seasick in a rowing boat on the boating lake in our local park. You hear lots of stories about cruises that go wrong – decoration not finished, staff on strike, poor standards of cleaning – that sort of thing. And I'm not too sure about being stuck on a ship with hundreds of other people. You'd never get any privacy.'

Discuss which of the customers you think would be **most** suited to a cruise holiday and which one would be **least** suited.

Cruise ships vary in size. The *Carnival Destiny* is over 100,000 tons and can carry more than 3,000 cruise passengers. However, there are a number of much smaller cruise ships carrying fewer than 300 passengers.

Cruise vessels are labour intensive. This means it takes a lot of people to carry out all the jobs needed to make the cruise a success. It has been estimated that on average there is one member of staff for every two passengers on a cruise ship.

Cruises are popular in Europe and in North America. Table 3.3 shows some of the ports where cruises often begin and some of the destinations they visit.

Cruises along some of the world's best known rivers are also popular. Good examples would be the Nile, the Amazon, the Rhine and the Mississippi.

Departure points	Destination
Florida (e.g. Miami, Tampa, Fort Lauderdale, etc.) Puerto Rico Jamaica	Caribbean islands
Los Angeles San Francisco	Mexico Panama Canal Alaska
Hong Kong Singapore	Hawaii Tahiti New Zealand Australia Japan
Southampton	Mediterranean Canaries trans-Atlantic
Dover Harwich Amsterdam Copenhagen	Norway Sweden the Baltic
Dover	Around Britain
Southampton New York Los Angeles	World cruises

Table 3.3

Activity 3.7

1 Make a copy of a blank outline map of the world.

2 Mark on it some of the main cruise routes shown in Table 3.3.

3 List as many reasons as you can think of to explain why these particular routes are popular.

4 Write a short report explaining the range of different types of cruise available and saying what type of markets you think each type is meant to appeal to.

Short and long haul destinations

So far we have looked at types of places to visit, such as the seaside or the country. These types can be found in many different parts of the world. In other words another thing people have to decide is whether they want a holiday in:

the UK (for people living in the UK these would be called domestic holidays);

somewhere in Europe;

somewhere in the rest of the world.

In Chapter 2 we looked at how distance and travelling time affects where people choose to go.

Some popular holiday destinations for people living in the UK include:

Part of the world	Examples of popular holiday destination areas
UK	Devon, Cornwall, the Isle of Skye, the Lake District, the Norfolk Broads, Snowdonia
Rest of Europe	Provence (France), Tuscany (Italy), Costa del Sol (Spain), the Tyrol (Austria), the Balearics (Majorca, Minorca, Ibiza)
Rest of the world	Florida, the Caribbean, Thailand, Goa (India), The Gambia

Holidays where a flight is needed to get you to the destination are often divided into two types – short haul and long haul tourism. These terms refer to the amount of time it takes to fly to the destination. Long haul tourism is usually used to describe destinations where the flight takes longer than 5 hours.

A long-haul destination – Sydney, Australia

1 Use an atlas to find out where the following popular tourist destinations are:

Bali	Hawaii
Nice	Marrakech
Amalfi	Orlando
Acapulco	Hong Kong
Athens	Marbella

2 Use the scales given in your atlas to estimate how far these destinations are from the UK.

3 If modern passenger aircraft cruise at about 500 miles per hour, work out roughly how long you think it might take to fly to each of these destinations from the UK.

4 Read the short descriptions below, taken from holiday brochures, of four of these destinations:

Bali – The climate in Bali is pleasant all year-round. The scenery is varied, including palm-fringed beaches, tiny villages and hills covered in patterns of rice terraces. The island is a cultural delight, offering a huge variety of temples, festivals, dances, crafts like silver jewellery, woodcarving and batik. The people of Bali are gentle and friendly and take a pride in welcoming guests.

continued

continued

Marrakech – This city was once the centre of an empire stretching from Senegal to Spain. Nowadays it is the major city of the south of Morocco. Its ochre walls date from 1127. The city has many examples of ancient monuments and beautiful gardens and has a very busy market. The city has a dramatic setting because of its closeness to the majestic Atlas mountains.

Hong Kong – Hong Kong is well known for wonderful shopping, excellent hotels and superb food. However, there is far more to see and do than that. In the New Territories and the outlying Islands you can see what rural China used to be like. There are plenty of sporting activities, such as golf courses and horse racing. Street markets sell everything from caged birds to Chinese medicines.

Acapulco – Acapulco is Mexico's best known international resort. It has a string of beautiful sandy beaches lapped by the deep-blue waters of the Pacific Ocean and ringed by lofty mountains. The city is modern and lively. All kinds of watersports are available during the day and a wide range of night-time entertainments is on offer.

If you were thinking about booking a holiday in one of these places, make a list of the questions you would want to ask the travel agent before deciding that it was the best choice for you. For example, you might want to ask what kind of health precautions were necessary.

Providing tourism products and services

4

Tourist information

Even when holiday-makers have arrived at their chosen destination, there are still products and services which they need. Perhaps the most important thing they want is information.

Here are some questions they might ask:

Where is the railway station?

What time does the bank open?

How much does it cost to get into the zoo?

Are there any rooms available at the Grosvenor Hotel?

Is the swimming pool heated?

Can we park near the craft market?

Can we hire a guide?

How old is the castle?

Most information tourists need falls into one of these groups:

- ✪ **Asking for directions**
- ✪ **Wanting to know opening times or times buses and trains arrive or depart**
- ✪ **Questioning the cost of things**
- ✪ **Wanting to buy tickets or book accommodation**
- ✪ **Checking what attractions and facilities are provided for visitors**
- ✪ **Asking where they can buy things**

Tourist Information Centres

One place tourists may go to look for information of this kind is a **Tourist Information Centre**.

These centres may be found in a number of different places:

- ✪ **In the high streets of historic towns**
- ✪ **In airports and railway stations**
- ✪ **In large retail stores**
- ✪ **Inside tourist attractions**
- ✪ **In a public library**

Tourist Information Centres are found in many different places

Exercise 4.1

For each of the types of information listed below suggest two questions which different tourists might ask in a Tourist Information Centre.

Type of information	Examples of questions asked
asking for directions	1 2
wanting to know opening times or times buses and trains arrive or depart	1 2
questioning the cost of things	1 2
wanting to buy tickets or book accommodation	1 2
checking what attractions and facilities are provided for visitors	1 2
asking where they can buy things	1 2

In order to provide this information people who work in a Tourist Information Centre can look in a number of different places:

- ✪ **A computer database of local accommodation**
- ✪ **Train and bus timetables**
- ✪ **Maps**
- ✪ **Guide books**
- ✪ **Telephone directories**
- ✪ **Hotel directories**
- ✪ **Entertainment guides**
- ✪ **Local newspapers**
- ✪ **Leaflets published by local attractions**

Inside a Tourist Information Centre

A lot of requests for information in Tourist Information Centres are about finding a place to stay for the night. Many TICs provide a service which involves finding and booking a local hotel or guest house which meets the needs of the person making the enquiry. Some TICs will also contact other TICs to make a room reservation in the place the tourist intends to stop the following night.

Activity 4.1

Choose a town or village close to where you live which does not have a Tourist Information Centre.

1   Discuss the possible reasons why there is no TIC there at present.

2   Make a list of all the sources of information in the area which would be useful in answering the sort of questions visitors might ask.

3   Choose a suitable place inside which a small TIC might be opened.

4   Either draw a sketch or a floor plan of the interior of this TIC, with some notes explaining why you think it should be designed and set out in this way.

Tourist attractions

Attractions provide interest, pleasure or entertainment for visitors. They are often what persuade people to visit a particular destination. For example, most people visit Orlando because they want to spend some time at Disneyworld.

There are a number of different types of attractions. Some of these are just natural features of a place, such as:

- ✪ **A sandy beach**
- ✪ **Snow-covered mountains**
- ✪ **A river valley**

The reason most people visit Orlando, Florida

Other attractions have been built specially for tourists. These include:

- ✪ **A theme park**
- ✪ **A swimming pool**
- ✪ **A leisure centre**

Some attractions were originally intended for another purpose but have become tourist attractions. Examples include:

- ✪ **A castle**
- ✪ **A church**
- ✪ **A pottery**

Exercise 4.2

The table below divides attractions into a number of different groups and gives three examples in each group.

Add two further examples of your own in each group.

Natural features	Entertainments	History
1 a sandy beach	1 a cinema	1 a castle
2 mountains	2 a disco	2 old city walls
3 a river	3 a bingo hall	3 a famous battlefield
4	4	4
5	5	5
Sports	**Industry**	**Arts and crafts**
1 a golf course	1 a glassware factory	1 a pottery
2 a swimming pool	2 a mining museum	2 an art gallery
3 a tennis court	3 a city farm	3 a jeweller's shop
4	4	4
5	5	5

Apart from the attractions which are natural features, most attractions raise money from visitors. They do this by:

✪ **Charging admission**

✪ **Selling products associated with the attraction**

✪ **Charging for tours of the site**

✪ **Providing catering services or selling franchises for other businesses to operate catering services on the site**

Appeal of different attractions

Tourist attractions change as people's interests change. Shopping was once thought of as being a necessary task in order to get basic food and clothing. For many people it has become a leisure activity they enjoy. Large shopping complexes like Meadowhall in Sheffield or the MetroCentre in Gateshead were built with the idea that they would attract many visitors from outside the area.

Shopping centres can include tourist attractions

Other places, such as cathedrals, began life with purposes which have been overshadowed by their appeal as visitor attractions. Westminster Abbey has to cope with more than two million visitors a year. This creates some problems for those who wish to use the building for its original religious purpose.

Places become tourist attractions for many different reasons. There are many country houses in Britain which attract visitors. These may be attractive because they are surrounded by landscaped gardens or because they contain valuable furniture, furnishings and art. Many of these country houses were originally private homes. Often they were opened to the public as a means of raising money to pay for the high costs of repairs and maintenance. Some were passed on to organisations like the National Trust in people's wills.

Places become tourist attractions for many different reasons

Even things like films and television can help to create tourist attractions. For example, people who have enjoyed particular TV programmes may choose to go and look at the place where it was filmed. Coronation Street is so popular with viewers that a tourist attraction, Granada Studios Tours, has been built around the set where the programme is filmed. Visitors can walk down the Street and have a drink in the Rover's Return pub. Other places are popular with visitors because they are associated with favourite books or their authors.

Exercise 4.3

1   Match up the television programmes in Column **A** with one of the tourist attractions in Column **B**.

2   Choose *three* other television programmes which you know are set in a real place.

List some ways in which the place where the programme is set might use this fact to try and attract more visitors.

A	B
1 Cheers	**a** the town of Holmfirth in Yorkshire
2 Inspector Morse	**b** Granada Studios Tours
3 Neighbours	**c** North Yorkshire Moors
4 Last of the Summer Wine	**d** a bar in Boston, USA
5 Coronation Street	**e** pubs and colleges in Oxford
6 All Creatures Great and Small	**f** Melbourne, Australia

Events

Events often attract visitors who would otherwise not have thought of going to a particular destination. Examples might include:

✪ **Sports competitions (e.g. the Olympic Games, the soccer World Cup)**

✪ **Carnivals (e.g. Rio de Janeiro, Trinidad)**

✪ **Musical performances (e.g. rock concerts, opera in Verona)**

✪ **International conferences and exhibitions (e.g. World Summit on the Environment)**

✪ **Festivals (e.g. Cannes Film Festival)**

Guides

There are many places people visit where knowing what you are looking at makes the experience more interesting. This could include visits to:

✪ **A city centre**

✪ **A river trip**

✪ **A church or cathedral**

✪ **A museum or art gallery**

✪ **A stately home**

✪ **A castle or other historical site**

✪ **A place where products are made, e.g. a vineyard**

A guided tour

Information about important people and interesting stories linked with the site can help people to understand what they are looking at, as well as keeping them entertained.

Activity 4.2

Choose an example in your area of one of the places listed above where the presence of a guide might make the visit more interesting.

1   Make your own visit to this place and list the things you think visitors would like to know about it.

2   Draw up a list of places where a tour guide could find the information to enable them to talk about the things you listed in **1**.

3   Write out a short speech which you think the tour guide should make at the beginning of a group's visit to the place you have chosen.

4   Make the speech to other students who have visited this site and collect their comments about whether they thought it would have improved their visit.

Tours

Tourists may not wish to spend their whole holiday in the same place. Most destinations give them opportunities to go on tours to various other places of interest. Tour services are offered by different types of transport providers. Coach tours are probably the most common. Other popular short tours include:

- ✪ **River and lake cruises**
- ✪ **Harbour cruises**
- ✪ **Steam train rides**
- ✪ **Hot air balloon trips**
- ✪ **Light aircraft or helicopter flights over spectacular scenery**
- ✪ **City tours in open horse-drawn carriages**

Walking tours around city centres are becoming more popular. Many of these are based on a particular theme. For example you can take a literary tour around Dublin, visiting places linked with famous writers like James Joyce and Sean O'Casey. A rather different tour is a night time walk around parts of London associated with Jack the Ripper. The *Oxford Ghost Tour* promises similar frightening experiences.

The Oxford Ghost Tour

Discover the dark side of Oxford's past in a spine-chilling guided walking tour of the city's streets, colleges and pubs. Tremble to the sinister tales of:

- ☞ Oxford's own vampire
- ☞ The headless king
- ☞ The haunted pubs & colleges
- ☞ Witchcraft and sorcery

and much much more.

Where? Tour starts from the Oxfam shop on Broad Street.

When? Every night at 9.00 p.m.

A spine-chilling attraction

An important part of any tour is the itinerary, or the route the tour takes. Among the things a good tour should include are:

✪ **Places of real interest to see**

✪ **A good balance between travelling and sightseeing**

✪ **A comfortable form of transport**

✪ **Good views for all passengers**

✪ **Information which can be understood by a range of passengers**

Activity 4.3

1   Choose four places of interest in a town or city close to where you live.

2   Prepare an itinerary which would take visitors to all of these places of interest, including a place where tours start and finish.

3   Research the travelling times between each of these places of interest and then estimate how long you think it would take for visitors to look around each place of interest.

4   Write some accurate timings into your itinerary, showing when the tour will start, how long will be spent in each place of interest and what time the tour will end.

Souvenirs

Tourists often buy goods to take home with them. They may have a number of reasons for buying these products. It may be:

✪   **To remind them of the destination they visited**

✪   **To give as presents to friends and relatives**

✪   **To decorate their homes**

✪   **To contribute to the local economy in the destination**

Some of the most common souvenirs which people buy are:

Souvenirs for sale

jewellery	furnishings
ornaments	food and drink
clothes	illustrated books
art and pottery	

Written destination guides often emphasise the range and quality of souvenirs which can be bought there. A range of unusual products can help to make the destination

Shopping in a Moroccan Market

sound more exotic. The following extract describes things which can be purchased in Morocco:

Strolling through the souks (markets) is a wonderful feast for the senses. And the pleasure is all the greater when you decide you are looking for a ring, a sword stick, a carpet, a pair of slippers, a wicker basket or rare and fragrant spices . . .

Every region has its specialities:

RABAT for embroidery and carpets; **SALE** for pottery.

CASABLANCA for leather work and Mediouna carpets.

MEKNES for carved wood, animals in metal inlaid with silver thread and mosaics.

FEZ, the craftwork capital, is famous for its pottery in Fez blue, copper trays and leather work.

In **MARRAKECH** the leatherwork is also very fine. You can see shoemakers sewing the slippers in the ancient tradition. The region is also famous for its incredible range of spices and the quality of its Berber carpets.

SAFI has its subtly coloured pottery with their amazing impression of relief, **TAZA** for its carpets woven by the Ait-Benhaddou Berber tribe, and at **ESSAOUIRA**, jewellery and marquetry as well as weaving, brassware and embroidery.

Methods of buying souvenirs are not the same in every country. In many countries there is still a tradition of bargaining over the sale of goods (bartering). A suitable price is agreed by a discussion in which the buyer makes offers below the orginal asking price until it reaches a level which the seller is willing to accept for the item.

Activity 4.4

Choose a town or city close to where you live which is not well known for tourism.

1 Discuss the main types of visitor the town or city seems to you to attract.

2 Outline three ideas for souvenirs which might be bought by any of the visitor types you discussed in task **1** of this activity.

3 Sketch a design for one of these souvenirs.

4 Compare your design with other similar souvenirs which you can already buy in local shops and suggest a price range which you think people might be willing to pay for the finished product.

Catering

Most visitors to tourist destinations need catering services. If they are staying in a hotel, meals will be provided on the premises. For those staying in self-catering accommodation or who have half board arrangements there is a need for a variety of eating places. The kind of catering services they want will depend on a number of factors, especially:

✪ **How much they are willing to pay**

✪ **How much time they have**

✪ **What style of food they prefer**

In many tourist destinations the local cuisine is one of the factors which attracts people. In Table 4.1 there are some examples of well known dishes which are linked with particular destinations visited by tourists.

Other destinations are associated with local drinks (Table 4.2).

Airport food

Food as a tourist attraction

In ...	A popular dish is ...	Which consists of ...
Greece	moussaka	minced meat, aubergines, tomatoes and cheese
Mexico	tortilla	a flat maize cake eaten with a variety of hot fillings
Hungary	goulash	a stew of beef, vegetables and paprika
Morocco	couscous	steamed wheat often served with meat and vegetables
Indonesia	rijstafel	a rice dish served with a variety of other foods

Table 4.1

In ...	A locally made drink is ...	Which consists of ...
Portugal	port	a wine, usually red, which has been strengthened by adding alcohol
Somerset, UK	cider	an alcoholic drink made from apples
China	rice wine	a drink made from fermenting rice
Caribbean	rum punch	a drink usually made from rum, syrup and lime juice
South West France	Armagnac	an alcoholic drink made in a similar way to brandy

Table 4.2

Exercise 4.4

Match the popular dishes in Column **A** to the countries listed in Column **B**:

A	B
Paella	Germany
Fondue	Italy
Quiche lorraine	Russia
Pizza	United States
Sauerkraut	Spain
Bortsch	France
Waffles	Switzerland

Exercise 4.5

Choose a tourist destination in your region and pick a site which is available for development. Someone is planning to set up a new food outlet in the destination. These are the ideas they have come up with so far:

★ A salad, soup and sandwich bar

★ An ice cream parlour

★ A fish and chip shop

★ A tea shop

1 Discuss which of these suggestions you think would have the best chance of being profitable.

2 Outline a proposal of your own which you think would be attractive to visitors.

Entertainments

Unless they have chosen to stay in a remote place, people on holiday have come to expect that there will be entertainments provided for them in a destination.

Entertainment products may be put together specially to appeal to tourists. For example:

- **Seaside resorts often have summer variety shows**

- **Overseas resorts often offer dance performances for tourists**

Other forms of entertainment, such as cinema or theatre, are available in destinations both to tourists and to the local community.

Examples of entertainment and their links with tourism are shown in Table 4.3.

Type of entertainment	Links with tourism
Cinema	Most tourist resorts have cinemas; in some places tourism has encouraged the development of facilities offering open air film shows
Theatre	Theatres tend to be found only in reasonably large towns. They may have seasons where performances are meant to appeal particularly to tourists
Music concerts	These may feature classical, popular or traditional music. Concerts by internationally famous performers often attract overseas visitors
Opera	Opera performances can be heard in many parts of the world. Some tour operators sell package holidays with tickets for important opera performances included
Dance	Dance entertainment includes both watching dance performances and going to facilities like discos, night clubs and dance halls
Cabaret/comedy/shows	Shows including music, comedy, dance and other variety acts are often put on in the summer at traditional tourist resorts

Table 4.3

Entertainment at a seaside resort

Exercise 4.6

Suggest a suitable evening entertainment for each of the following tourists:

1   A group of 20 French students on an exchange visit to a school or college in your region.

2   Twenty residents of a home for elderly people on a coach tour stopping for the night at a hotel in your region.

Sports and leisure facilities

People on holiday have a lot of leisure time to fill. Many are quite happy just to relax but others need to be more active. They may want to try a new activity out of interest or they may feel it is more healthy to get some exercise even while they are on holiday.

Most tourist destinations provide facilities where sports and leisure activities can take place. Some of these are developed mainly for use by tourists but others have shared use with the local community.

Another reason for developing these facilities is that they are mostly under cover. Indoor activities mean that there are still things for visitors to a tourist destination to do, even if the weather is bad. Not all sports and leisure facilities are indoors. Many tourists choose a destination because it is well known for offering particular types of outdoor activity.

Indoor facilities

- ✪ **Sports centres**
- ✪ **Indoor tennis courts**
- ✪ **Tenpin bowling alleys**
- ✪ **Skating rinks**
- ✪ **Pool and snooker clubs**
- ✪ **Swimming pools**
- ✪ **Squash courts**
- ✪ **Dance halls**

A sports centre is used by tourists and the local community

Outdoor facilities

- ✪ **A golf course**
- ✪ **Tennis courts**
- ✪ **Bowling green**

An outdoor facility for locals and tourists

- ✪ **Horse riding stables**

- ✪ **Canoeing and rafting equipment and tuition**

- ✪ **Supervised climbing activities**

- ✪ **Ski slopes**

- ✪ **A diving school**

- ✪ **Water skiing and windsurfing tuition**

Exercise 4.7

An aerobics instructor working in a seaside resort thinks there might be a demand for aerobics classes from people on holiday.

Discuss the following questions:

1 What methods could she use to try and find out how much demand there might be?

2 What would be the best ways of advertising the classes?

3 What facilities and equipment would she need to make the classes a success?

4 What differences would there be in running classes for tourists from running classes for local people?

5 How would she work out how much to charge people for attending the classes?

6 What problems do you think she might come up against in trying to get classes for tourists established?

The demand for leisure facilities

The demand for leisure facilities varies across different age groups. More often than not discos will be attended by younger audiences than those who attend bingo sessions. Very physical activities, like playing rugby or mountaineering, become more difficult as you grow older. Tastes in leisure activities change too. Young people would have been much more likely to learn ballroom dancing 60 years ago than they would today. Figure 4.1 shows how the popularity of the cinema varies among different age groups.

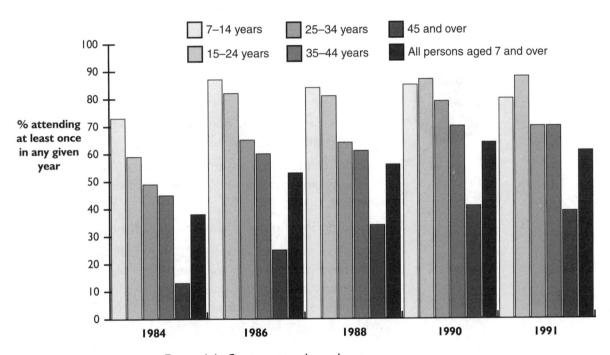

Figure 4.1 Cinema attendance by age

People's choices about which leisure facilities to use also depend on the kind of job they do. Two examples of the influence of work on leisure facility use are:

✪ **People on high incomes can afford to use more expensive facilities**

✪ **People in part-time jobs have more leisure time available**

Many leisure facilities suffer from considerable variation in demand, depending on the time of year. For example, professional sports grounds are most heavily used during the summer or winter, depending on the main sports which take place in them. For obvious reasons open air facilities like swimming pools and bowling greens are likely to get heavier use in summer than in winter. Indoor facilities may be more popular during the colder months. Facilities like restaurants and clubs often attract more people over holiday periods, especially at Christmas and the New Year.

Exercise 4.8

1 Discuss what trends can be seen in the figures for cinema attendance in Figure 4.1.

2 What reasons can you suggest for these trends?

Activity 4.5

1 Make a photocopy of a map of the area surrounding your school or college.

2 Divide leisure facilities into a number of categories, e.g. spectator/participant; arts/sports; free/making a charge.

3 Mark the location of all leisure facilities on the map.

4 Prepare a short presentation, to be made to representatives of your local authority leisure or recreation department, identifying the demand for leisure facilities in your age group and the extent to which existing facilities meet this demand.

Managing funds in a leisure facility

All leisure facilities have to keep a record of their income and expenditure. Each year they prepare a *budget*, predicting how much they think they will receive from different sources and proposing how this income should be spent. They then monitor this process throughout the year to ensure that they are meeting their expected income targets and not exceeding their planned spending. Unexpected rises or falls in income or expenditure will generally result in adjustments having to be made to the original budget plans.

Facilities where a number of activities take place need more careful analysis of income and expenditure. An arts centre may find that its weekly film shows are very popular and therefore profitable, but its theatre performances are more costly to put on and are attracting very small audiences. The centre will have to balance what its policy says about providing a variety of arts experiences against its need not to show large losses. In other words showing more films and fewer plays might be more profitable, but might also cater for a smaller section of the local community.

Exercise 4.9

Each of the following items is either income for a football club or expenditure.

Place a tick against those which are income and a cross against those which are expenditure:

Police presence at matches		Sales of replica shirts	
Players' salaries		Accommodation for away matches	
Gate receipts		Fees from TV companies	
Sponsorship		Programme sales	
Having programmes printed		Cost of relaying pitch	

The location of leisure facilities

Since many people live in urban areas the location of the majority of leisure facilities is within easy reach of population centres. In other words most theatres, swimming pools, sports grounds, museums and restaurants are found in or near towns and cities.

Transport is important. Leisure facilities are usually in places which can be reached by both public transport and by private cars. Most people use leisure facilities which are local. However, facilities which are seen to be different from or better than others, such as Alton Towers, can attract people who live a long way away.

The fact that most people now have cars means that facilities like football grounds are now being built on out of town sites. People can reach them by car, park at the ground and cause less disturbance to people living near the ground.

Different regions' leisure facilities will also reflect the culture of the region. Rugby league coaching is more likely to be available in Wigan than in Windsor. There are more crown green bowling facilities in the north of England than in the south. Greater London and the South East had 233 golf courses in 1991 while there were only 121 in Wales. Similar variations can be found with arts facilities. Cities which have built up a reputation for music, such as Birmingham with the City of Birmingham Symphony Orchestra, attract both music lovers and other musical events. The same is true of places which support major annual arts and music festivals, such as Edinburgh, Cheltenham and Aldeburgh.

Exercise 4.10

Examine the table below based on Sports Council figures for 1991. It shows the number of swimming pools, sports halls and golf courses in different regions of England, Wales and Scotland.

1   Why might there be fewer sports facilities in the Sports Council's Northern region than elsewhere?

2   What factors might account for the large number of golf courses in Scotland?

3   In which regions do you think swimmers and gymnasts would have the greatest choice of facilities to use?

4   What other figures would you need to have in order to show whether there was a fair supply of leisure facilities in each region?

Region	Swimming pools	Sports halls	Golf courses
Eastern	96	113	164
East Midland	128	110	101
Greater London	122	158	233*
Northern	52	84	100
North West	241	177	180
Scotland	125	n/a	385

continued

continued

Region	Swimming pools	Sports halls	Golf courses
South East	68	88	233*
Southern	83	124	103
South West	117	276	126
Wales	114	120	121
West Midlands	148	208	122
Yorkshire & Humberside	232	169	141

*Greater London & South East combined

Management of leisure facilities

Many decisions have to be taken each day in a leisure facility. In a small facility one person may take many of the decisions. In larger facilities there may be a number of working teams based on departments or on different work areas. For example a large leisure complex may have:

- **A catering team, often staffed by a contract catering company**
- **A team of fitness instructors and coaches**
- **A team of receptionists**
- **A team of administrators**

Each departmental team will report to a senior manager.

An example of a departmental structure is given in Figure 4.2.

The relationship between the different levels in a management structure depends to some extent on the personalities involved. Some managers may prefer to be seen as a senior employee who passes on instructions to more junior staff. Others prefer a more informal approach, adopting what is sometimes called an 'open door' style of management. Managers preferring an informal style would be more likely to consult other staff when making decisions.

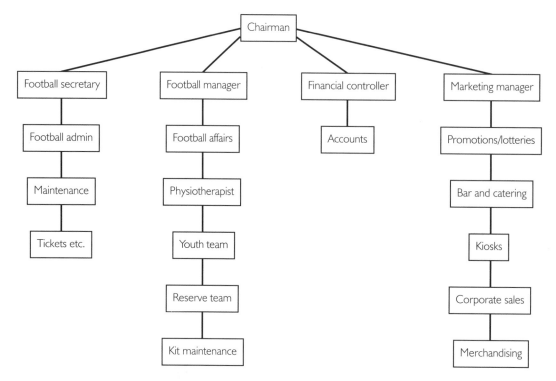

Figure 4.2 *The management structure at Swindon Town Football Club*

Activity 4.6

1   List three jobs which people carry out in a leisure centre.

2   For each of these jobs write down two important decisions which their managers might need to discuss with them. For example, where a new item of fitness equipment should be placed in the gym.

3   Role play discussions between a manager and another employee in which (i) the manager gives instructions about what should be done (ii) the manager discusses the best approach with the employee.

Staffing leisure facilities

Leisure facilities need different types of staff:

⊙ **People who work directly with the public, such as receptionists**

⊙ **People who work 'behind the scenes', completing such vital tasks as maintenance and administration**

Leisure facilities need both highly skilled workers and those with little specialist training or qualifications. For example a garden centre may employ both sales assistants with basic retail training and managers with horticultural qualifications and extensive experience of working in garden or nursery environments. Garden centres need sales staff, administrators, plant experts, maintenance staff and people to carry out relatively unskilled tasks like cleaning and moving stock about.

Employment at a leisure facility

Managers of leisure facilities often have advantages in recruiting new employees. The environment of a theme park or a cinema, for example, is associated with enjoyment and it seems natural to think that it would be fun to work there. However, this also means that employees have to be capable of appearing cheerful even when they don't feel that way.

Table 4.4 shows some of the answers of leisure facility managers who were asked what they thought were the main advantages and drawbacks of the kind of work their employees did:

Leisure facility	Attractions	Drawbacks
professional football club	• excitement of match days • variety	• long, often unsocial hours • many tasks physically demanding
large garden centre	• friendly working environment • opportunity to acquire wide range of knowledge and skills	• working in the open in all weathers • lifting and carrying required
local theatre and arts centre	• meeting people out to enjoy themselves • seeing a range of performances	• unsocial hours, especially evenings • financial pressures of performance-related pay
city centre business catering unit	• short working hours • free food • better than average job security	• low pay • occasional difficult customers
local authority sports and leisure centre	• a sociable atmosphere • chance to develop own hobbies/ skills at work • varied, active work	• evening and weekend work • shift work • can include some menial tasks such as cleaning equipment

Table 4.4

Larger facilities may use computer software to help them manage their staff needs. These computerised labour management systems can help to manage staff rosters, payrolls and personnel files. They can be used to get information about things like:

✪ **The time individual tasks take to complete**

✪ **The skills which tasks require**

✪ **The hours employees have worked**

✪ **The performance of staff involved in sales**

As with other resources, the cost of spending more on employing more staff has to be set against the improved service and profits it is capable of bringing.

Exercise 4.11

Draw up your own table, like Table 4.4, showing what you think are the main advantages and disadvantages of working in:

★   A cinema

★   Horse riding stables

★   A tenpin bowling alley

★   A golf club

Setting prices in leisure facilities

Deciding how much to charge for admission to a leisure facility is not easy. The facility needs to make enough money to meet its costs. If it is a facility which is meant to provide for a local community, such as a leisure centre, it will have to make sure that its prices are set at a level which different groups in the community can afford.

The main factors which a leisure facility has to think about in setting its pricing policy are:

> *Is the facility expected to run at a profit?*
>
> *Does it receive any subsidies?*
>
> *How variable is the demand for use of the facility?*
>
> *What kind of costs does the facility have to meet?*
>
> *What are people willing to pay for the use of both other similar facilities and other alternative recreational activities?*
>
> *What do competitors charge?*

There are advantages and disadvantages to different pricing policies.

Low prices

Attract new customers
Increase users in off-peak times

May reduce income
More difficult to provide good service
May be seen by customers as cheap

High prices

Can attract richer people
Can develop luxury surroundings

Customers will expect high standards
Many people will not be able to
afford it

Variable prices

Can attract different groups, such as
senior citizens, young children, school
groups or the unemployed
Attract more people in quiet periods

Harder for customers to work out
prices
Harder for staff to work out prices

Special prices

(e.g. season tickets, membership schemes)

Would encourage customer loyalty
Would encourage advanced booking
Can bring in income early
Reduces administration cost

Needs more advanced planning

The Haydon Leisure Centre can be hired for children's parties. At the moment four Party Packages are available. This is how the leaflet advertising them describes what is offered:

Birthday Party Package for YOU!

It's the greatest way to hold a children's party. No need to worry about noisy children at your home. No need to say 'Watch the carpet!' Why not bring the noise and mayhem to the Haydon Centre and get the most out of our Party Packages!

PARTY PACKAGE 1

Full use of the Flexi Hall (sports hall), to play and organise your own games at an incredible:

Price £15.60

PARTY PACKAGE 2

Full use of the Flexi Hall, plus a member of staff to organise and supervise a variety of fun-packed activities and games.

Price £20.60

PARTY PACKAGE 3

Full use of the Flexi Hall plus the Centre's own bouncy castle – a real crowd puller!

Price £25.60*

PARTY PACKAGE 4

For a 'Mega-Party' this package has got the lot! Fun and games in the Flexi Hall plus the bouncy castle and a member of staff to arrange and supervise fun activities and games. This is the party everyone wants to be invited to and all for

Price £30.60*

For Party Packages 3 and 4 the bouncy castle must be erected and dismantled within the period of your booking.

The Centre has received a number of requests for additional Party Packages, including demands for (a) longer sessions (b) more than one staff member (c) use of a junior swimming pool.

1   Write descriptions of *three* new Party Packages which the Haydon Centre could offer.

2   Suggest a price for each Package, explaining why you have arrived at these figures.

3   List any factors which you think would lead the Centre to consider changing its prices for any of the Party Packages which it offers.

Health and safety in leisure facilities

Leisure facilities have a responsibility for the health and safety of three main groups of people:

✪ **Their own staff, including permanent, temporary and visiting repair or maintenance staff**

✪ **Their customers, including their use of the premises themselves and any equipment they make use of**

✪ **Members of the public who are close enough to the facility to be affected by activities or repairs taking place in or around the facility**

The Health and Safety at Work Act 1974

The Health and Safety at Work Act is very important in making sure that all workplaces are aware of their responsibilities. Table 4.5 describes the main responsibilities which this Act puts on management and employees:

Role	Responsibilities
Management	The provision and maintenance of plant, systems and premises in a safe condition
	Ensuring that there is no risk to health or safety in the handling, using or storing of articles and substances
	The maintenance of places of work, entries and exits in a safe manner
	The provision and maintenance of a safe working environment, including facilities and arrangements concerned with staff welfare
	Ensuring that all staff are adequately informed, instructed, trained and supervised in workplace health and safety regulations
	The publication of an up-to-date health and safety policy
	Consultation with health and safety representatives
Employees	Considering the health and safety of themselves and others who may be affected by their actions
	Working in co-operation with employers to ensure that the conditions of the Act are fulfilled

Table 4.5

continued

Role	Responsibilities
Employees	Correctly handling and maintaining plant, fixtures and fittings provided, in the interests of health, safety and welfare
	Reporting any health and safety risks or accidents

Table 4.5

Exercise 4.12

For each of the seven responsibilities of management listed in Table 4.5, discuss a specific course of action which the manager of each of the following leisure facilities might have to take in order to ensure good health and safety practice:

The manager of a city centre night club, housed in a basement

The manager of a tenpin bowling centre with its own restaurant

The manager of a Lido, offering windsurfing, waterskiing, diving instruction and swimming facilities

Some aspects of health and safety in a leisure facility would be checked by an Environmental Health Officer. For example the Officer might inspect leisure facilities for any of these reasons:

✪ **To check that water supplies and swimming pools are clean and wholesome**

✪ **To grant licences to centres where there are live animals, such as equestrian centres**

✪ **To check retail premises to ensure that their products are safe and hygienic**

✪ **To advise on the likely local impact of new leisure developments, such as sports stadia or night clubs**

✪ **To investigate accidents in non-industrial workplaces**

Exercise 4.13

Match the type of leisure facility in Column **A** to the possible risks and hazards to safety given in Column **B**.

A Leisure facility	B Risk or hazard
1 health and fitness centre	**a** <ul><li>injury caused by lifting heavy items</li><li>paths made slippery by watering plants</li><li>careless use of trolleys, e.g. overloading</li><li>movement of fork-lift vehicles</li><li>misuse of tools, e.g. secateurs</li></ul>
2 theme park	**b** <ul><li>overcrowding or crowd disturbance</li><li>fire</li><li>poorly maintained crash barriers</li></ul>
3 cave open to the public	**c** <ul><li>defective fitness equipment</li><li>misuse of fitness equipment</li><li>over-exertion on fitness machines</li><li>dehydration</li><li>viewing gallery</li><li>excessive time spent in sauna or under sunbeds</li></ul>
4 swimming pool	**d** <ul><li>passenger behaviour on rides</li><li>mechanical safety of rides</li><li>contaminated food</li><li>condition of paths and steps</li><li>increased motor traffic</li></ul>
5 football stadium	**e** <ul><li>slippery floors</li><li>contaminated water</li><li>swimmers getting into difficulty in or under water</li></ul>
6 garden centre	**f** <ul><li>low ceiling</li><li>uneven steps and floors</li><li>steep or slippery paths</li><li>deep shafts and deep underground lakes</li></ul>

Leisure facilities and the local community

Some leisure facilities are built to meet community needs. Community centres are particularly valuable in localities with an elderly population, especially where public transport is infrequent. Such facilities provide not only a range of activities, but also serve the important social function of providing a meeting place for people who could otherwise easily become isolated.

Leisure facilities can benefit the local community by:

✪ **Improving people's health**

✪ **Providing them with new interests**

✪ **Enabling people to meet new friends**

Facilities may set up events and activities to improve their reputation in the local community. Here are some examples:

Facility	Community activities
Professional football club	*Players visiting local hospitals* *Coaching sessions for young children* *Charity fund-raising at matches* *Donating prizes to raffles*
Public house	*Charity collections* *Organising outings for disadvantaged groups* *Taking part in charity and sponsored events*
Garden centre	*Providing work placements for students* *Running competitions for children* *Offering prizes for horticultural competitions*
Amateur cricket club	*Coaching sessions for children* *Use of ground and facilities for charity events* *Selling charity lottery tickets*

Activity 4.8

1   Identify a leisure facility near your home and suggest *three* ideas for events or activities, which it might put on to try and support the local community.

2   For *one* of these events or activities write a press release intended for local newspapers, highlighting both the event or activity itself and the ways in which the facility feels it can serve the local community as a whole.

Promotion of leisure facilities

Promotion is used to give potential customers an idea of what goes on in a leisure facility, both in terms of the range of activities and services it offers and the atmosphere which is created inside it.

Demand for many leisure facilities is seasonal and promotion is needed to stimulate sales during off-peak periods. There is a wide range of leisure activities which customers can choose to take up. They may choose to do without leisure activities altogether when economic conditions are hard. Both these factors make promotion important for leisure companies wishing to do better than the facilities they are competing against.

Promotion of a leisure facility is concerned with communicating its range of services to people who might be interested. The most common ways in which a facility might do this are by:

Advertising – local and national newspapers, magazines, trade press, posters, hoardings, bus sides, local and national radio, television, direct mail.

Sales promotion – point of sale material, prizes, price discounts, promotional evenings, in-store promotional events, branding of products.

Publicity and public relations – press visits, press releases, special events, product placement in film and TV programme locations, community projects and charity donations.

Table 4.6 shows the way a number of leisure facilities use different kinds of promotion to attract people to special events.

Leisure facility	Methods used to promote events
garden centre	• handouts at the tills • signs on approach roads • posters displayed in the centre • a forthcoming attractions display board • local press and radio advertising
community centre	• posters in local public libraries • advertisements in tenants' newsletters • word of mouth • posters in other community venues
health and fitness centre	• newsletter to members • posters displayed in the centre • recommendations from trainers/consultants to individual members
local authority leisure centre	• advertising in local press and on local radio • direct mail using purchased lists • presentations given in local schools and colleges • leaflets in local public libraries and local government offices

Table 4.6

Exercise 4.14

Read the following account of how leisure facilities use different kinds of promotion. Match words from the list which follows with the spaces in the account.

booking; press; premieres; retail; coverage; reviews; recommend; logo; performances; direct

A professional football club can promote its name through the sale of leisure wear and other items bearing the club's (1)_____. Promotion is often a two-way process for professional sports with a high profile. Live television (2)_____ means that other companies will pay the host club to position advertisements at strategic points around the ground.

Garden centres will often mount promotions with companies whose products they sell. For example, Kennedy's Garden Centre recently worked jointly with Fisons to promote both the sale of hanging baskets and the plant food which Fisons (3)_____ for feeding these baskets.

Leisure facilities often used computerised (4)_____ systems to generate address lists which they can use for (5)_____ mail promoting new products or services. Sports centres may use this process to advertise leisure goods which they offer for sale in a (6)_____ centre.

continued

continued

Cinemas and theatres will generally advertise in the local (7)_____. They may also pay to have information about dates and times of (8)_____ listed in weekly entertainments guides and on television information systems like Ceefax and Prestel. Journalists may be invited to new plays and films (9)_____ in the hope that they will give wider coverage by writing reviews of what they have seen. This can backfire of course if the (10)_____ are not very complimentary!

Staging events in leisure facilities

Much planning has to take place before leisure facilities can put on events for the public. In order to run an event managers have to decide:

- ✪ **When the event should be held**
- ✪ **What the programme for the day should be**
- ✪ **What additional staffing arrangements need to be made**
- ✪ **What safety and security measures will be required**
- ✪ **What resources will be needed and who is to supply them**
- ✪ **What publicity the event will need**
- ✪ **What space, facilities and equipment will need to be available**
- ✪ **What the budget for the event should be and what income it should raise**
- ✪ **What planning is needed for things which might go wrong**

Exercise 4.15

1 Choose *one* of the following events which might be staged at a leisure facility:

an art exhibition; an indoor hockey tournament; a New Year's Eve dinner and dance; an antiques fair; a carnival parade; a sponsored half-marathon

2 Make a list of the planning decisions which you think would need to be taken in the weeks leading up to the event.

3 Discuss which of these decisions would need to be taken early, which ones would be necessary in the run up to the event, and which ones could be taken immediately prior to or even during the early stages of the event itself.

Planning for things which might go wrong, sometimes called contingency plans, is important. This might include:

✪ **Bad weather**

✪ **Traffic congestion delaying arrival or admission**

✪ **People causing a disturbance**

Events need proper resources if they are to be a success. Resources include:

People

Materials and equipment

Locations

Funds

The table **below** shows examples of these types of resource:

People	Extra stewards; extra sales staff; car park attendants; extra catering staff
Materials and equipment	Public address system; temporary crash barriers; cutlery and crockery; children's inflatable play areas; additional seating; food and drinks; mobile telephones for stewards
Locations	Room; hall; auditorium; outdoor open space
Funds	Grants; loans; sponsorship

Activity 4.9

1   Think of an event which your school or college could put on in order to attract greater use of its facilities by the local community.

2   List what extra equipment you would need to hire for this event.

3   Sketch a floor plan of the area where you would hold the event and mark on it:

Admission and exit points

The access routes for motorists and pedestrians

Parking facilities

Where equipment and materials would be delivered and collected

Where equipment in the area might need to be moved and stored

Discuss any possible resource problems you might have in putting on this event.

Events need a schedule to make sure that everything runs smoothly. They will also need a certain amount of paperwork, including things like:

- ✪ **The timings and venues of different activities, in the form of a schedule for staff and perhaps a programme for people who attend the event**

- ✪ **The roles and responsibilities of participating staff**

- ✪ **The working hours of staff involved, usually written up as a staff roster**

- ✪ **The prices to be charged for admission and for any goods offered for sale**

- ✪ **The current level of ticket sales, usually indicated on seating plans and by the number of printed tickets still available**

- ✪ **Detailed client requirements, including likely number of attenders, indicated on booking forms**

- ✪ **Where and when any outside catering supplies are to be delivered, the main details of which are often part of the formal catering contract**

- ✪ **Instructions for event participants, e.g. treasure hunt clues, quiz answer sheets**

The health and safety of people attending events is also very important. Table 4.8 shows some of the practical measures leisure facilities can take to improve safety and security.

Risk	Practical measures to counter it
fire	• smoke alarms and sprinkler systems • clearly lit labelling of fire exits • staff training in use of fire extinguishers and evacuation procedures
theft	• night time security guards • floodlighting of secluded areas • alarm systems linked to local police station • video surveillance • a strong safe with a time delay lock • increasing advance and credit card bookings to reduce amount of cash
accidents	• first aid training for staff • increasing checks on machinery and equipment • increasing investment in maintenance • clear warning signs • conducting a safety audit

Table 4.8

Read the schedule of events for a Craft Fair to be held at Easthampton Town Hall on Sunday, 27th November 2000:

CHRIST✟MAS CRAFT FAIR

Skilled exhibitors selling hand crafted gifts

Demonstrations

Refreshments ❄ Easy parking ❄ Well signposted

OAK LANE, EASTHAMPTON

OPEN 10 AM – 5 PM

Adults £1 Children & Senior Citizens 50p

Enquiries Tel: 0666 34567

Special Events and Demonstrations

Time	Event	Venue
10.30 a.m.	Under-12 painting competition	Compton Room
10.30 a.m.	Pottery demonstration	De Vere Room
11.00 a.m.	Illustrated talk: 'Antiques – spotting the genuine article'	Vauxhall Room
11.00 a.m.	Reupholstery demonstration	Main hall
11.30 a.m.	Demonstration of jewellery-making	Main hall
11.45 a.m.	Wine-making demonstration and wine tasting	Vauxhall Room
12.15 p.m.	Illustrated talk on dried flowers	Compton Room
2.00 p.m.	Pottery demonstration	De Vere Room
2.00 p.m.	Children's Treasure Hunt	Compton Room
2.15 p.m.	Visit by Lord Mayor and Lady Mayoress	Tour of all rooms
2.30 p.m.	Radio Easthampton Live!	Main hall
3.00 p.m.	Demonstration of jewellery-making	Main hall
3.00 p.m.	Illustrated talk: 'Antiques – spotting the genuine article'	Vauxhall Room
3.30 p.m.	Reupholstery demonstration	Main hall
4.00 p.m.	Grand lottery draw	Main hall

1 Discuss any problems you think might arise from this schedule.

2 How do you think each of the following might plan a visit to the Craft Fair:

A mother with two children, aged 6 and 8 years, wishing to find out about possible craft activities she can try at home

A small party of eight elderly American tourists with a couple of hours to spare in the afternoon

An unemployed school leaver looking for ways of earning some money

3 The Lord Mayor and Lady Mayoress indicate that they will spend up to an hour at the Fair, 10 minutes of which will be taken up by the Mayor's speech. Both visitors are keen to see a range of demonstrations. What rescheduling do you think would be necessary to meet with their wishes?

continued

continued

4 Due to an oversight the Vauxhall Room has been pre-booked by another organisation and all activities which were due to use it must be transferred to either the De Vere Room or the Compton Room. Reschedule these activities so that they do not clash with any other uses of the rooms or any other similar activities.

5 At the last minute, Bill de Kuyt and Netta Scarfe, the authors of a new book about making children's toys, offer to appear for an hour, selling signed copies. Identify what you think would be the best time for this and give reasons for your choice.

Evaluation is an important part of running an event. A facility needs to have a way of measuring whether the event was a success or not. They could do this by:

- ✪ **Counting the number of people who attend**

- ✪ **Adding up the amount of money spent and comparing this with the costs of putting on the event**

- ✪ **Comparing the numbers attending and the money spent with the same figures for different events**

- ✪ **Adding up the amount of coverage which the event gets in the newspapers**

- ✪ **Giving out questionnaires to be filled in by people attending the event**

A leisure facility might set some targets to help its managers decide whether an event had been successful. They might aim to:

- ✪ **Increase the number of visitors on a particular day**

- ✪ **Increase the number of club members**

- ✪ **Increase the amount spent on food and drinks**

- ✪ **Improve on the attendance at a similar event**

- ✪ **Raise an agreed amount for a charity**

- ✪ **Attract a new business sponsor**

Exercise 4.16

Brainstorm the ways in which a leisure facility could evaluate the health, safety and security measures it had taken for a particular event.

Which of your ideas could be measured and how would you carry this out?

Who provides leisure facilities?

Leisure and sports facilities are usually provided by one of the following:

✪ **Local or national government (the public sector)**

✪ **Commercial companies (the private sector)**

✪ **Voluntary organisations (the voluntary sector)**

Table 4.9 shows some examples of the way the different sectors developed facilities and what their reasons were for doing so.

The three sectors also often work together to develop new leisure and sports facilities.

For example a local authority may own a sports centre but it is quite likely to be managed by a private management team which has to meet certain targets set out in a contract. Cleaning and catering within the centre may in turn be contracted out to other private specialist companies.

New leisure facilities are often funded by a mixture of grants from local or national government or even from European funds, and investment by private companies. Even voluntary organisations, such as amateur sports clubs, may seek the status of a charity. This means that they can carry out various business activities in order to raise funds.

Leisure/sports facility	Developed by ...	Because ...
swimming pool	local government (public sector)	they have a responsibility to provide leisure services for the local community
bowling alley	leisure company (private sector)	they exist to make a profit for the owners and shareholders
cricket club pavilion	fund-raising by club members (voluntary sector)	the members want to make the game more enjoyable and they want to attract new players

Table 4.9

Amateur sports clubs may seek charitable status

1 Make a copy of a street map of a small tourist destination.

2 Mark the location of all leisure facilities on the map.

3 Ask the other students in your group:

What activities and facilities they look for on holiday

How much time they spend on these

4 Discuss how well the tourist destination you chose would meet the needs and interests of your student group.

5 Prepare a short presentation, to be made to representatives of the local authority leisure or recreation department in the destination, explaining:

The demand for leisure facilities in your age group

How much existing facilities meet this demand

What new facilities would help to meet the demand

6 Discuss who might consider providing the types of leisure facility you have chosen and what benefits or drawbacks they would need to take into account before they invested in such developments.

Working in travel and tourism

5

The importance of customer service

Customers are vital to the tourism industry because they are the people who buy its products and services. Tourism businesses need the money they spend in order to:

- ✪ **Cover the costs of setting up and running the business**

- ✪ **Develop new and better services and products**

- ✪ **Make money for their owners and the people who have invested in them, such as shareholders**

Good customer service is also important in keeping customers and making sure they do not go and buy the same products and services somewhere else. It costs a company more money to attract new customers than it does to sell to existing customers. This is because existing customers already know what the products and services are like and therefore do not need the same levels of advertisement and promotion to draw their attention to them.

Good service in the travel and tourism industry

We all know if we are getting good service or not. Think about the examples below:

The importance of customer service

OH WELL, MOPPING UP WILL PASS THE TIME WHILE YOU WAIT FOR YOUR FOOD.

A travel agent promises to send out tickets in two days but they arrive a week later.

A customer waits 40 minutes for their meal to arrive in a restaurant.

A phone call to an airline is put on hold for 10 minutes.

A cabin on a cruise ship has not been thoroughly cleaned before departure.

A visitor in a wheelchair is unable to get into the upstairs rooms of a country house.

All of these things would cause disappointment. In order to make sure customers are not lost because of events like this, many companies set customer service standards for their employees. These standards can cover all areas of the business but might include things like:

❂ **The accuracy of documents sent out to customers**

❂ **The speed with which the telephone is answered**

❂ **The levels of hygiene and cleanliness**

❂ **The dress and appearance of employees**

❂ **How complaints are dealt with**

Customer service in travel and tourism is about things like:

❂ **Observing and listening to find out about different people's needs**

❂ **Taking trouble to make sure these needs are met**

❂ **Making people feel welcome**

- **Keeping people entertained**
- **Ensuring that people are safe**
- **Taking responsibility for sorting out problems**
- **Providing accurate and reliable information**

Exercise 5.1

Here are some examples of customer service:

Type of customer service activity	Examples
observing and listening to find out about different people's needs	1 Travel sales consultant makes notes of a telephone request from a customer for a special anniversary holiday. 2
taking trouble to make sure these needs are met	1 Travel sales consultant rings a hotel to ask for special diet for a customer with health problems. 2
making people feel welcome	1 Overseas rep for tour operator hosts a welcoming party for new arrivals in a destination. 2
keeping people entertained	1 Staff at a tourist attraction, wearing fancy dress, talk to children queuing to go on rides. 2
ensuring that people are safe	1 Tour operator puts two drivers on coaches taking holiday-makers on long journeys. 2
taking responsibility for sorting out problems	1 Airline cabin crew ask passengers to exchange seats to give more space to a young mother and child. 2
providing accurate and reliable information	1 Travel sales consultant provides computer printout of choice of flight reservation times and prices. 2

Give a similar example in each case of the same type of customer service being offered in a different travel and tourism situation.

Meeting different customer needs

Not all customers have the same needs. Each of the following may be a customer of a travel and tourism business:

- ✪ **A visually impaired person**
- ✪ **A vegetarian**
- ✪ **A person who cannot speak the local language**
- ✪ **A mother with a young baby**
- ✪ **A person who is afraid of flying**

Meeting the needs of the customers

Some travel and tourism businesses, like airlines and hotels, attempt to find out these special needs at the time the customer makes a booking. Others, especially facilities like museums or leisure centres, use permanent design features to try and provide for all types of visitor. Table 5.1 gives some examples.

A/An ...	Might help the needs of ...	By ...
art gallery	*a blind person*	displaying sculptures which visitors can touch
conference centre	*a vegetarian*	having a vegetarian choice on all menus sent to customers
airport	*a person who cannot speak the local language*	having signs and announcements in other languages
tourist attraction	*a mother with a young baby*	providing free push chairs and changing facilities
tour operator	*a person who is afraid of flying*	offering alternative transport routes to the destination

Table 5.1

Handling complaints

Customer complaints are important for two main reasons:

- ✪ **They show a company how good its customer service is**
- ✪ **They tell its managers which areas of the company's activities need improving**

If complaints are not handled well, the result will be not just lost customers, but the reputation of the company may suffer as well.

There are many things that can go wrong in the travel industry. Take the example of people travelling by air. They might have to face:

- ✪ **Flight delays**
- ✪ **Lost luggage**
- ✪ **Food which they don't like**
- ✪ **Not enough leg room**

While these things do not happen all the time, customers tend to remember when things go wrong.

There are a number of stages in handling a complaint well (Table 5.2).

Stage One	listening carefully to what the customer is complaining about
Stage Two	making sure the details of the complaint are agreed
Stage Three	explaining what actions can be taken to deal with it
Stage Four	carrying out whatever action has been agreed
Stage Five	telling the customer and work colleagues what has been done

Table 5.2 The five stages of dealing with a complaint

Look at the following telephone conversation:

Tourist:	The pool in our villa was filthy and there was no equipment to clean it.
Tour operator:	I'm very sorry to hear that, madam. (*apologises*) It obviously wasn't what you, or we, would expect. (*shows sympathy*) What was the name of the property you stayed in and when were you there? (*asks questions to check details*)
Tourist:	The Bella Vista apartments in San Ferromagiagno. We came back last week.
Tour operator:	Right. I will be in touch with the property owner to make sure that this doesn't happen again. I'd also like to offer you a £50 refund, as well as our apologies. I hope it didn't spoil the rest of your holiday. Is that acceptable? (*accepts responsibility for the problem and takes positive action immediately*)
Tourist:	Yes. That will be fine.

Activity 5.1

The chart below suggests some Dos and Don'ts when dealing with customer complaints.

Do ...	Don't ...
... listen to what a complaining customer has to say	... walk away from a customer with a problem
... try to take a friendly approach to calm an angry customer	... get into a loud argument with a customer in public
... explain the things you know can be done about the complaint	... promise action which may not be allowed or possible
... where it was unavoidable, give an explanation of the causes of the problem	... blame other colleagues or the company system

continued

continued

1   Develop four role plays, each one in a different tourist context (e.g. in a hotel, on an aeroplane, waiting for a ride in a theme park attraction), in which a customer makes a complaint.

        Act out two versions of each role play. In the first version the tourism employee follows the advice in the **Do . . .** column of the table above. In the second version they follow the actions listed in the **Don't . . .** column.

2   Make a list of the feelings and reactions which the customer has as a result of the two different kinds of treatment they receive.

The range of jobs

Working in the tourism industry is about providing for the needs of visitors. These needs are:

Accommodation and catering – hotels; guest houses; caravan parks; camp sites; holiday centres; restaurants; pubs; cafes

Travel and transport – airlines; coaches; rail; travel agents; tour operators

Leisure and visitor attractions – theme parks; zoos; leisure centres; cinemas; night clubs

Heritage and the countryside – museums; art galleries; religious buildings; historic houses; national parks; urban parks

A job in the tourism industry

To meet these needs the tourism industry employs people of all ages, with a wide variety of skills and experience. Many of the jobs involve face to face contact with visitors. The list below shows some of the jobs done by people in the tourism industry:

air cabin crew

airport staff

art gallery assistant

bar staff

box office staff

caravan and camping park staff

car hire staff

catering manager

chef

coach driver

computer operator

entertainer

fast food service staff

gardener

guesthouse owner

hotel manager

housekeeper

leisure centre assistant

lifeguard

local authority tourism officer

local tour guide

motorway services staff

museum assistant

nightclub and disco staff

night porter

park warden/ ranger

pool assistant

porter

publican

public relations officer

railway staff

receptionist

reservations assistant

resort representative

restaurant manager

retail assistant

security staff

sports centre staff

taxi driver

theatre manager

tour guide

tour operator

tourist information centre staff

transport staff

travel agency sales consultant

visitor attractions manager

waiter/waitress

zoo and wildlife park staff

Let's look at each of these four main areas of work in turn:

Jobs in accommodation and catering

The main areas of work in these two sectors are shown in Table 5.3.

Accommodation	Catering
housekeeping	food service
reception	food preparation
bar service	cookery catering management
conferences and banqueting	
hotel management	

Table 5.3

Accommodation

Housekeeping – looking after hotel rooms, including cleaning and changing towels and bed linen.

Reception – welcoming guests, answering enquiries and dealing with customers' bills.

Bar service – serving drinks and making sure that supplies of drinks in good condition are always available.

Conferences and banqueting – providing for the needs of business groups during meetings held in hotels and conference centres.

Hotel management – dealing with all aspects of the running of a hotel, including finance, marketing, customer relations and levels of service.

Catering

Food service – bringing food from where it is cooked to the place where the customers will eat it or take it away from.

Food preparation – planning and cooking a variety of meals.

Catering management – planning and organising a catering service, including buying supplies, preparing and serving food, organising staff and making sure the whole operation makes a profit.

Exercise 5.2

1 List a range of tasks which you think have to be carried out in the normal day-to-day running of a hotel.

2 Look at the different areas of work shown in Table 5.3. Place each of the tasks you listed in **1** into one of these different areas of work.

Jobs in travel and transport

The main areas of work in these two sectors are shown in Table 5.4.

Travel	Transport
tour operator	airlines
travel agent	coach companies
	rail companies
	ferry companies

Table 5.4

Travel

A **tour operator** – works with a number of suppliers (businesses which provide transport, accommodation and leisure) to arrange, advertise and sell package holidays. The work may be based in the UK, for example arranging flight, rail, ferry and accommodation details or taking reservations. It could also involve working overseas, for example negotiating with accommodation providers or acting as a holiday rep in a resort.

A **travel agent** – advertises and sells holidays put together by tour operators, usually from shop premises. They advise customers about which holiday packages will best suit their interests and their budget.

Some tasks carried out by travel agency sales consultants are:

- ✪ **Keeping reservation records up to date**
- ✪ **Maintaining filing systems**
- ✪ **Stamping brochures**
- ✪ **Maintaining supply of racked brochures**
- ✪ **Assessing customers' needs**
- ✪ **Answering questions from clients**
- ✪ **Advising on holiday choices available**
- ✪ **Checking prices and availability of holidays with tour operator**
- ✪ **Advising on visa and health precautions**
- ✪ **Supplying foreign currency and travellers' cheques**
- ✪ **Supplying holiday insurance**
- ✪ **Receiving payment**
- ✪ **Issuing tickets**

Transport

Transport companies employ people to do many different kinds of work. Some jobs – like an airline pilot – need a very high level of skills and qualifications.

Table 5.5 shows the different types of transport company and gives some examples of the types of jobs they have available.

Type of travel	Types of employer	Some examples of jobs
road	● coach companies ● car hire firms	drivers, office staff, coach tour guides, mechanics
rail	● national rail network ● private railways	drivers, technical staff, office staff, on-board catering, ticket sales
air	● airlines ● airports	pilots, air cabin crew, air traffic controllers, technicians, airport staff
sea	● cruise lines ● ferry companies ● canal boat hire	chief officers, pursers, medical officers, entertainments officers, office staff

Table 5.5

Some jobs are highly skilled

Exercise 5.3

Read the following description of what a member of an air cabin crew does:

'People think working as part of an airline cabin crew is always fun and exciting. In fact it involves a lot of hard work. Tasks often have to be carried out in difficult conditions. For example, there is not much space for them to carry out their work.

Passengers get bored and uncomfortable and so complain. They may feel ill or be frightened of flying. The air cabin crew have to stay cheerful, even though they may be tired. On long flights the crew may have to work very long spells without a break.'

1   What sort of problems do you think air cabin crew might have to deal with during a long flight?

2   What sort of qualities and skills do you think somebody would need in order to make a good member of an air cabin crew?

3   What kind of training do you think would be the best way of preparing air cabin crew to deal with the kind of problems you listed in **1**?

Jobs in leisure and visitor attractions

This may involve working in any of the attractions shown in Table 5.6.

Tourist attractions	Sports and leisure attractions
theme parks	leisure centres
zoos	swimming pools
castles	health resorts
country houses	outdoor centres
archaeological sites	tennis courts

Table 5.6

People working in *tourist attractions* might be employed as:

Gardeners

Ride operators

Entertainers

Guides

Craftspeople

Security officers

People working in *sports and leisure attractions* might be employed as:

Receptionists

Fitness trainers

Beauticians

Lifeguards

Sports instructors and coaches

Maintenance and ground staff

An entertainer at a tourist attraction

In the UK, work in tourist attractions is often seasonal, perhaps lasting from Easter to the end of October. Some of the jobs available are linked to special events, like car rallies, pop concerts and craft fairs. These may only last for the period of the preparation and holding of the event.

Some areas of this sector use voluntary staff to cover the times they are open or events are taking place. Examples would include:

- **Voluntary staff acting as guides or wardens in rooms of smaller country houses open to the public**

- **Voluntary turnstile operators and stewards supervising the entry and movement of spectators at football matches**

Activity 5.2

1 Arrange a visit to a local tourist attraction or sports and leisure attraction.

2 Make a list of all the jobs you think have to be carried out to make the attraction a success.

3 Decide whether you think each of these jobs is a full-time job or would only take a part-time employee to finish.

4 Note which of the jobs would be seasonal and which might be needed all year round.

5 Estimate how many people you think it would take to run the attraction.

6 Try to find out how many people actually work there and why this number is higher or lower than the number you estimated in **5**.

Jobs in heritage and the countryside

Many jobs are linked with heritage and the countryside. They include people who work in:

Museums

Art galleries

Churches and cathedrals

Historic houses

National Parks

Urban parks

They might be employed to:

✪ **Sell souvenirs to visitors**

✪ **Provide guided tours**

✪ **Keep an eye on valuable exhibits**

✪ **Issue tickets and collect admission fees**

✪ **Grow and plant flower beds**

✪ **Build new footpaths to prevent damage**

Exercise 5.4

1 List some of the possible advantages and disadvantages of working in a cathedral shop.

2 List the different kinds of knowledge you would need to have in order to be good at this job.

Skills and personal qualities

Valuable skills and qualities for recruits to the tourism industry

A group of employers in the tourism industry was asked recently about the skills they thought are most important for anyone thinking about working in the industry. They came up with a list of basic skills and qualities. Many of these are skills or qualities which employers in other industries would also be looking for in new recruits.

- ✪ **Good verbal communication, both face to face and on the telephone**
- ✪ **At least a basic level of accurate written communication**
- ✪ **Careful listener**
- ✪ **Looks smart and presents themselves well**
- ✪ **Good timekeeper**
- ✪ **Can plan tasks and work towards targets**
- ✪ **Dependable**
- ✪ **Enthusiastic and motivated**
- ✪ **Wants to develop and improve their own career prospects**
- ✪ **Must be able to work well in a team**
- ✪ **Some basic knowledge of information technology use**
- ✪ **An ability to sell**
- ✪ **Acceptance of good health and safety practice**
- ✪ **Willingness to accept responsibility**

These skills are all very general. Other skills required might have more direct links to tourism. For example, depending on the type of job being applied for, candidates might be expected to:

- ✪ **Know about laws like the Food Safety Act**

Many traditional skills are needed in the tourism industry

❂ Have a knowledge of the main transport systems in the UK

❂ Be able to understand how a computer reservations system works

Activity 5.3

1   For each of the skills and qualities listed above, discuss some of the things which might happen in different kinds of tourism business if employees did not possess these skills and qualities.

2   For each of these skills and qualities, plan a method of finding out whether a possible new recruit to a tourism business possessed them or not.

3   Try out some of your methods on other students to see if you think they have these qualities.

More developed skills

For people who have worked in tourism for a while or who are looking for jobs with more responsibility, employers will look for more developed skills. These include things like:

❂ **Numeracy**

❂ **Literacy, including understanding written materials and writing clearly and accurately**

❂ **Using computer technology for work tasks, communication and information retrieval**

❂ **Practical selling ability**

❂ **Problem solving, especially to help customers**

❂ **Working within cost limits**

❂ **Familiarity with basic reference sources**

❂ **Understanding principles of marketing**

❂ **Ability to speak a foreign language**

❂ **Ability to organise projects and events**

Problem solving

Here is an example of part of a job description which describes the qualities and skills needed for a particular job.

Information receptionist for Tourism Information Centre

Wales Tourist Board

Qualities needed

ⓘ **Pleasant and confident personality**

ⓘ **Good communicator**

ⓘ **Able to act on own initiative**

ⓘ **Methodical**

ⓘ **Literacy and basic numeracy**

ⓘ **Enthusiasm for selling Wales as a destination**

ⓘ **Smart**

ⓘ **Patient**

Skills needed:

ⓘ **Detailed knowledge of the locality, of Wales and of the UK in general**

ⓘ **Ability to communicate through public speaking, displays and foreign languages**

ⓘ **Able to show good customer care**

ⓘ **Can use manual and electronic systems of storing and retrieving information**

ⓘ **Able to research useful information**

ⓘ **Knowledge of stock control, cash handling and providing management information, including statistics**

ⓘ **Ability to manage office procedures**

Read the list of job opportunities offered by a tour operator, First Choice.

Summer Resort Representative   Minimum age: 21

As our guests' plane touches down, your job starts. Transferring them to and from the airport, selling excursions, arranging Welcome meetings, supplying information, solving problems, writing reports. . . . The list goes on. Now you see why we ask for flexibility and stamina!

2wentys Representative   Minimum age: 20

Our 2wentys guests are not looking for a quiet life! A fun atmosphere and an action-packed programme are the order of the day (and night). So leadership skills, loads of energy, huge credibility and a personality to match are essential requirements. If you can think on your feet while standing on your head, so much the better.

Childrens' Representative   Minimum age: 19

Keeping our younger guests occupied and safe is a full time job, requiring a qualification in childcare or youth work, or at least 2 years' related experience. We're looking for people who can provide fun and entertainment for younger children as well as for teenagers. Stamina, imagination and creativity won't go amiss, either!

Administrators   Minimum age: 21

Getting the right people to the right place at the right time demands first-class administrative co-ordination. Not to mention excellent communication skills, numeracy, computer literacy and, usually, a second language. This job is not your typical 9–5 office work.

1   For each one of the four jobs listed here make a list of the skills and qualities which you think would be needed to do the job well.

2   Write down some questions which you think an interviewer might ask applicants for each of these jobs.

3   Discuss what activities you have been involved in which you would describe if you were being interviewed for one of these jobs. What skills did they help you to develop?

Personal qualities

There are many personal qualities which employers, including those in the tourism industry, look for. They hope their staff:

> *are honest;*
>
> *have good manners;*
>
> *are friendly;*
>
> *are confident;*
>
> *are well organised;*
>
> *have a sense of humour;*
>
> *are reliable;*
>
> *get on well with other people.*

Think about what the following examples show about the importance of some of these personal qualities:

1 A customer enters a travel agency, wanting advice about suitable ski destinations for beginners. Two counter clerks carry on a conversation they are having about where they should go for the office Christmas party. The customer eventually interrupts with a request for information and one of the clerks points to where the ski brochures are. The two staff continue their conversation.

Good manners are essential

2 A hotel resident asks for decaffeinated coffee with their dinner and is told by the waiter that they have run out. The same thing happens the following evening and a different waiter says the hotel doesn't serve it because there isn't much demand for it.

Honesty is the best policy

3 A car park attendant at a popular country house open to the public says that a car with a couple and their elderly parents, both of whom walk with the aid of a stick, must be parked in the next space in the row being filled, even though this means the car is a long way from the house entrance.

Be thoughtful about other people's needs

The ability to get on with other people

4 An attendant in an art gallery sits in a corner, chewing gum and reading a book. A visitor asks about a painting and the attendant says there is information in the guide book on sale in the gallery shop. She then shouts at two small children, loud enough for their parents to hear, that if they can't keep quiet then they had better leave.

In all of these examples an employer would not be pleased with the employee's behaviour. In each case visitors would have been put off coming again. Each visitor might then go away and tell other friends and relatives about their experience, making it more likely that these people would not visit either.

More suitable ways of dealing personally with these four different situations would have been:

1 The agency could set up a training programme. This would show staff how to greet customers when they enter the shop, even if this means interrupting what they are doing. If they are dealing with another customer, they might say something like: 'Good morning . . . I'll be with you as soon as possible. Please do browse through the brochures or have a seat while you're waiting.'

2 A member of the hotel staff could have been sent out to a local grocer on the first evening to buy a jar of decaffeinated coffee. If it proved impossible to get something a customer asked for, the waiter should apologise and suggest some choices the guest might like to try instead.

3 The car park attendant should receive some customer care training. A sensible approach would have been to suggest a parking place nearer the entrance, or allowing the elderly couple to be set down by the entrance before parking the car elsewhere. The owners of the house could set aside parking spaces near the house for people with mobility problems.

4 A major part of the gallery attendant's job should be to provide information and this should be part of an employee's initial training. Children could be dealt with more tactfully. For example the attendant could sympathise with the parents about children getting a bit bored with art and could suggest other parts of the grounds or building which children might find more interesting.

Exercise 5.6

1 Which of the following do you think are good ways for staff in tourism facilities to begin conversations with visitors:

Excuse me . . .   Tickets, please . . .
Wait here . . .   Keep over to the left . . .
Is everything all right . . .   He/she's not here at the moment . . .
Have a nice day . . .   I don't know . . .
Hi . . .   What . . .
How's your meal . . .   Speak up a bit . . .
I won't be a minute . . .   Can I help . . .
Welcome . . .   Would you mind if . . .

2 For each of the beginnings you did not like, suggest another way of beginning the conversation which you think would make a better impression.

3 Many tourist attractions are visited by families with young children. What advice would you give to new employees about the ways they should react to and speak to young children?

Qualifications and training

Some jobs in tourism ask for particular qualifications from anybody who applies. These might include qualifications taken at school, such as:

- ✪ **GCSEs**

- ✪ **A levels**

- ✪ **GNVQs**

These can be achieved by passing examinations, completing coursework or by collecting a portfolio of evidence about assignments and tasks completed during the course.

Some jobs may also require vocational qualifications, such as NVQs. These are usually based on how people carry out different tasks at work. Each NVQ is linked to a particular occupation, such as travel services or tour operations. They can be gained through study at college, as long as there is some work placement activity included.

Exercise 5.7

Study the table of travel and tourism qualifications and then answer these questions.

1   What is the purpose of studying for a GNVQ in Leisure and Tourism?

2   What qualifications do you need to begin a GNVQ Intermediate Leisure and Tourism course?

3   What qualifications are available for people wishing to become air cabin crew?

4   Where would you go to study for a BTEC Higher National qualification?

5   What career would you be interested in if you applied to take an ABTOC qualification?

6   If you want to become a registered tour guide, who should you get in touch with?

7   Suggest two common ways of studying for an ABTAC qualification.

8   How long does it take to study for a degree in tourism?

continued

continued

Qualification	What jobs will these qualify me for?	What subjects & levels does it cover?	Where will I go to study for the qualification?
GNVQs (General National Vocational Qualifications)	The GNVQ will not qualify you for specific jobs but will provide a background for a wide range of jobs in Leisure & Tourism	Leisure & Tourism Levels: Foundation, Intermediate, Advanced	Any approved college or school
NVQ/SVQs (National/ Scottish Vocational Qualifications)	A wide range of jobs across the travel services and events sector	Travel Services Levels 2, 3 in: * Leisure and Business * Tour Operations * Commentaries & Interpretation for Tourism Level 3 (Supervisory) & Level 4 (Management) Other relevant NVQ/SVQs * Air Cabin Crewing * Events	Any approved college, training provider and company. The NVQ/SVQ assesses competence in the workplace so a programme offered by a college or training provider must include work experience.
BTEC Higher National/First	The BTEC qualifications will not qualify you for a specific job but will provide background for a wide range of jobs in travel and tourism	* Business with travel and tourism * Travel and tourism * Leisure with travel and tourism Levels: First, National, Higher	Colleges of Further Education, 6th Form Colleges and Colleges of Higher Education
Degrees in Travel & Tourism	Degrees will not qualify you for specific jobs but will provide a background for a wide range of jobs in travel and tourism sometimes at a senior level	* Travel and Tourism * Tourism * Business with travel and tourism * Tourism Management	Universities and Colleges of Higher Education
ABTAC (ABTA Travel Agents Certificate)	Leisure travel sales consultant	Major aspects of leisure travel at Primary and Advanced levels	Any ABTAC Franchised college or college which offers ABTAC, self study programmes or while working in the industry
ABTOC (ABTA Tour Operators Certificate)	Relevant to working in reservations, customer support and resort operations	Major aspects of tour operations at Primary and Advanced levels	Details regarding courses of study are not yet available. The first exam will take place in December 1997. Contact the awarding body or local college for further details
Air Fares & Ticketing Qualifications	The Air Fares & Ticketing qualification will not qualify you for a specific job but will be useful for jobs in retail and business travel and work with airlines	Quoting fares, completing tickets and providing information and advice Basic to Advanced levels	Private training providers, colleges and airlines
GBTA and City and Guilds Certificate in Business Travel	Business Travel Consultant up to management level	Major aspects of business travel introductory to management - 4 levels	This qualification is not yet widely available. Contact awarding body for further details
Registered Guide Qualification	Guides for sites, historic buildings, places and tours (walking and coach)	Major aspects of guiding in UK - one level	Regional Tourist Boards
RSA Coach Tour Guides Certificate & Diploma	Working as a walking, site and coach tour guide	Based on equivalent to NVQ levels 2 to 3	Various colleges

What is the normal programme of study and how will I be assessed?	What entry qualifications will I need?	Who should I contact if I am interested?
A programme between 1 and 2 years with continuous assessment and unit tests	Foundation: no formal entry requirements Intermediate: normally 3 to 4 GCSEs grades A to F. Advanced: normally 4 GCSEs grades A to D	The Awarding Bodies: EDEXCEL OCR AQA Local colleges
A programme of work place assessment and where appropriate formal training	No formal entry requirements. Past experience and qualifications will be taken into account.	The Travel Training Company Training and Enterprise Council (TEC) Local Enterprise Companies (LEC) The Awarding Bodies: EDEXCEL OCR SCOTVEC Local industry Local colleges
One to two year programmes of study with continuous assessment and examinations	First: passes in GCSEs, eg. maths, english National: First or minimum one A level but other qualifications taken into account Higher: National or 2 A level passes	Individual colleges EDEXCEL
Normally 3 or 4 year programmes for under graduate studies, continuous assessment and examinations	2–3 A level passes in related subject. GNVQ Advanced. Other qualifications will be taken into account	Individual universities and colleges
Various programmes of study eg. evening classes, self study 3 hour examination	No formal entry requirements	The Travel Training Company Local colleges Local industry ABTAC Franchised Centres
It is expected that various programmes of study will be offered 3 hour examination at each level	No formal entry requirements	The Travel Training Company Local colleges Local industry
Training courses (various duration) or self study and up to 3 hour examination for each level	No formal entry requirements	The Travel Training Company Airlines Local colleges
Assessment is a combination of examination and performance assessment via a logbook. The management level qualification is assessed via examination and assignments	Whilst there are no formal entry requirements, experience and existing qualifications will be taken into account	Guild of Business Travel Agents OCR
Written and practical exams. Course of study varies according to region	No formal entry requirements. Potential candidates will be interviewed and asked to complete a test	Regional Tourist Boards Local Authorities
Length of programme varies	No formal entry requirements	

Working conditions

Working conditions are different in every job. Some of the areas to think about when describing the working conditions which apply to any job are:

- ✪ **What the actual workplace (the physical environment) is like**
- ✪ **How many hours have to be worked and at what times**
- ✪ **What the rates of pay are**
- ✪ **Whether employees receive any benefits that come with the job**
- ✪ **What pressures are involved in this particular kind of work**
- ✪ **Whether the job is a desk job or involves physical exercise**

In each of these areas, there are things which can make the job more difficult to do or which can make it more satisfying for the employee. For example:

The physical environment

work may be **indoor** or **outdoor**

there may not be much **space** to work in

equipment may be out of date

there may be good or poor **facilities** for staff

health and safety risks may be higher in some workplaces

The hours worked

may involve **weekend** and **evening** work

may involve **shift work**

some jobs may mean **early starts**

Huh! . . . Fed up with sitting behind a desk? Work in the great outdoors and meet lots of people . . .

there may be **off duty time** during the day (**split shifts**)

some jobs are **seasonal/part time**

The pay received

may only be **low pay**, especially at the start

some jobs offer **performance related** bonus or commission payments

some employees can earn **tips**

The benefits

accommodation is sometimes provided

low cost travel and holidays go with some jobs

some jobs offer **free use of leisure facilities**

The pressures of the job

many jobs have **peak periods** each day

some jobs, especially in transport and overseas, carry a big **responsibility for the safety of others**

with many competing companies, there is a pressure to increase **profitability**

external factors often mean quick changes to plans are needed

Exercise 5.8

Discuss the working conditions you would expect if you were employed as:

A zoo keeper

A member of an airline cabin crew

A Punch and Judy show operator

A chef

An entertainer on a cruise ship

Consider each job from the point of view of the physical environment people work in, the hours you think they might have to work, the benefits they might be offered and the pressures which come with each particular job.

Workplace Regulations set standards for the working environment.

ROOM SIZE
big enough to allow activities to be carried out safely

VENTILATION
proper supply of fresh air

LIGHTING
good enough to work by and avoid hazards

WORKSTATIONS
allow comfortable sitting position for any person

Standards applying to the workplace environment

Exercise 5.9

The following paragraph is about safety standards in the workplace. Fill in the blank spaces by choosing from the list of words below.

crowded; carpets; partitions; slippery; panel; overhead; guards; materials

Floors and passageways can be very dangerous. It is important to make sure that there are no torn (1)_____ or holes in the floor which could cause people to fall. In areas like kitchens, where the floors need to be cleaned regularly, it is vital to make sure people know if floors are wet and therefore likely to be (2)_____.

Wherever there is a chance of people falling over edges there must be (3)_____, rails or fences. This applies to all drops of more than 2 metres. Tanks and pits must be covered and any goods stored (4) _____ must be securely held in place.

Doors and (5)_____which you can see through can cause serious injury if people walk into them. They should be clearly marked to show that they are there and should be made of (6)_____ which are not likely to cause cuts and bruises if anyone collides with them.

Doors should open in the direction less likely to be (7)_____. If they open both ways they should have a clear (8) _____ so that you can see anyone approaching from the other side.

Activity 5.4

Design a poster intended to encourage food safety standards in a tourism workplace. You might use examples like a railway buffet car or a windsurfing equipment hire company.

Here are some examples of working conditions for a number of tourism industry employees:

Hotel manager

Hotel managers usually work long hours, often including weekends and evenings. They have to be ready to deal with problems and emergencies at any time. They are often provided with accommodation and meals, especially if they work for one of the bigger hotel groups.

Chef

Chefs usually work on a shift basis, including evenings and weekends. In a hotel the breakfast shift might start at 6.30 a.m. while in a restaurant the evening shift might not end until midnight. Some posts offer accommodation and free meals.

Holiday centre staff

Jobs at holiday centres often mean long hours and shift work, especially at peak season.

Many staff are on contracts for the season, perhaps working only from early March to November. Permanent, senior staff spend the winter months planning publicity, installing new attractions and generally maintaining the centre.

Seasonal jobs could be in security, entertainment, bars, restaurants, shops, kitchens or in accommodation services.

A few centres, especially those where the main attractions are under cover, are open all year.

A chef in his working environment

Cruise staff

Some cruise staff work on board ships while others are based in company offices.

Head office staff generally work normal office hours. Those involved in marketing the company's products will have to take part in evening and weekend promotions.

Sea-going staff have very flexible working hours. Days at sea can be busier than those in a foreign port, when most passengers go ashore.

On-board staff may work from 3 to 6 months at a time, followed by four to eight weeks' leave. While at sea, free meals and accommodation are provided.

Stewards and stewardesses

The hours of work will vary depending on where people are employed.

For instance, staff on cruise liners may work a 24-hour shift system for three or four months at sea, followed by four or more weeks' holiday. Time off to look around the foreign ports a cruise ship stops in may be given.

Ferry or hovercraft crew work varying shifts, depending on the length of the crossing. Accommodation and food are provided.

Train staff also work shift systems, which may include early starts, late finishes and weekend and bank holiday work. Staff may have to live near their base station.

All stewards wear uniforms, and most are given reduced-rate travel.

Resort couriers and representatives

Resort reps need to have good relations with hotel and restaurant staff and managers of tourist attractions. Although couriers are surrounded by people, they actually work on their own most of the time.

Reps and couriers may be asked to work at any time of the day or night. For example, couriers pick up passengers whenever they arrive and representatives may be on call 24 hours a day.

As the work is seasonal. Most reps and couriers earn most of their income during the summer months, while ski reps earn mainly during the winter months.

Historic property staff

Many historic properties are open only from Easter to October, and some staff are therefore employed on a seasonal basis, either full or part time.

For managers the summer is busy, welcoming visitors and dealing with special groups, coach parties and individual visitors. Winters are spent supervising maintenance, organising special events and publicity, and ordering new stocks of souvenirs.

Staff are normally required to work on a rota basis when the property is open, including weekends, although evening work is not normally required.

Activity 5.5

1   Select *three* job advertisements from the trade press offering employment in different travel and tourism occupations.

    Note any details in the advertisement which relate to pay and conditions.

2   List what you think are the advantages and disadvantages of each of these three types of employment.

3   Use careers books and other resources to make some notes about each of the three jobs you chose in **1**.

    Some of the topics you might be able to find out about are:

    Levels of pay

    Hours of work

    Any special benefits which come with the job

    What the working conditions might be like

    What training might be available

Applying for a job

Writing your CV

Most jobs advertised in travel and tourism expect people applying to complete application forms and send in a CV. A CV, or a curriculum vitae, gives a short account of your education and career. It usually includes information about:

Biographical details – name, address, telephone number, age, nationality

Qualifications – secondary school and further education attended and dates; qualifications gained and grades; training courses attended; useful skills developed (e.g. IT capability, clean driving licence)

Work experience – dates of previous employment; position held; duties and responsibilities; salary and reason for leaving. Present employer should come first; then others working back to your first job

Hobbies and interests – list interests relevant to the job; positions of responsibility held; membership of relevant societies/organisations

Referees – addresses and phone numbers of two previous employers or others who have experience of your qualities and abilities

Things to avoid in a CV

Don't include information they don't need to know, e.g. your weight

Don't include details which are not true or accurate because you will probably be questioned about them

Don't leave out reasons for leaving employment – they will probably be checked

Make sure your CV is neatly set out and does not contain spelling errors

Don't use poor quality paper

Letters of application

Employers who ask for a letter of application are usually looking for evidence to show that you have read the job description. The letter will usually give more detail about things in your CV, showing how they would make you a suitable candidate for the job. The job description shows you what duties and responsibilities you would be expected to carry out. Your letter is a chance to persuade the employer that you could carry them out well.

The letter of application may help to decide whether or not you get an interview. Important points to remember are:

✪ **The content of the letter should cover aspects of the job description**

- ✪ **The language of your letter should be clear and polite**
- ✪ **Your grammar and spelling should be accurate**
- ✪ **If a handwritten letter has been asked for, your handwriting should be neat**

Here is an example of a letter of application and a CV from someone applying for summer season work at North Point Leisure Park:

---

38 Craven Road
Tydin
Notts
NG7 8PR

20th March 1999

Ms Ira Crewe
Manager
North Point Leisure Park
North Point
Notts NG5 4GB

Dear Ms Crewe,

I am writing about your advert in the North Point Advertiser for Leisure Park staff for the coming summer season.

I am in my second year of a GNVQ Advanced Leisure and Tourism course at North Point College and I hope to work in the travel and tourism industry when I have finished my studies.

I already have experience of working with the public, am interested in a range of sports and can speak fluent French.

I am available for interview at any time.

Yours sincerely,

Michelle Charvet

Curriculum Vitae
Michelle Charvet
38 Craven Road
Tydin
Notts
NG7 8PR

Education 1992–1997

North Point Comprehensive School

GCSE: English (C); English Literature (B); French (A); Art (B)

GCE A level: French (B)

GNVQ: Leisure & Tourism (Intermediate) – Merit

Leading roles in three school drama productions.

Member of school hockey and netball teams.

North Point College

GNVQ: Leisure & Tourism (Advanced)

Secretary, Students' Union 1998–99

Employment

Tydin Public Library 1997–1998

Saturdays and early evenings. I dealt with enquiries (both face-to-face and using the computer system), cataloguing new books, displays and reading sessions for young children.

Bleakview Caravan Park Summer 1998

Duties included cleaning, cooking and running children's competitions in the on-site games room.

Activity
5.6

Discuss how suitable you think this letter and CV are for someone applying to work as a summer season employee at a Leisure Park.

Successful interviews

The majority of people appointed to jobs are successful as a result of having an interview. The interviewer will use questions, discussion and sometimes tasks to find out what applicants are like and whether they are suitable for the job advertised.

Here is some advice about interviews from the Personnel Manager of a major retail travel chain:

Try to make a good first impression, both through your appearance and through trying to find out something about the company you are applying to.

Be as honest and open as you can and admit it if you don't know something.

Listen carefully to the questions you are asked and don't be afraid to ask the interviewer to repeat anything you are not clear about.

Be ready to give examples from your previous school or work experience which show your own skills and personal qualities.

Make sure that you have a normal amount of eye contact with your interviewers.

First impressions are very important

Preparing for the interview

First impressions are very important. How you prepare for an interview may make a difference in terms of whether or not you get the job.

Exercise 5.10

Discuss which of the following suggestions are sensible preparation for an interview and which are not:

- ✪ Wearing a purple shirt
- ✪ Covering a visible tattoo with a plaster
- ✪ Taking an umbrella
- ✪ Eating garlic bread for lunch
- ✪ Taking your belongings in a plastic bag
- ✪ Tying back long hair
- ✪ Using strong perfume or aftershave
- ✪ Having a drink to calm your nerves
- ✪ Taking a clean copy of your CV with you
- ✪ Arriving 30 minutes early
- ✪ Chewing gum to keep your breath fresh

It is important to check beforehand how to get to the place the interview is being held in. You should also work out how long it will take to get there. You should take the company's telephone number with you in case you need to contact them for any reason.

To find out about the company you are going to, you could try writing to them, looking in your careers library or local public library, or searching on the internet.

The interview itself

Each interview is different but most interviewers will ask about:

- ✪ **Details of your CV**
- ✪ **Why this particular job interests you**
- ✪ **What your main achievements are**
- ✪ **What ambitions you have**

- ✪ What skills, interests and abilities you have

- ✪ Whether there are any questions you want to ask

Activity 5.7

1   Choose a job advertisement from a leisure or travel trade newspaper which looks as though it might be open to a school or college leaver.

2   Prepare a letter of application and CV which would be suitable to use in applying for this job.

3   Discuss the letters and CVs written by your group and decide which ones look the best.

4   Make a list of the good and bad points of the letters and CVs and make a new version of your own letter and CV which takes these points into consideration.

5   Make a list of some of the questions you think an interviewer for the job you have chosen might ask.

6   Find a partner to act as the interviewer and role play the interview so that you have to answer the questions you listed in **5**.

Do people and places benefit from tourism?

6

Tourism employment – more tourists means more jobs

Employment in tourist destinations depends both on the number of visitors and the amount of money they spend. If there is an increase in the number of visitors, this usually means there will be more tourism jobs available. The extra visitors will need somewhere to stay, something to eat and a range of things to do. If a new hotel is built they will need reception staff, porters, chambermaids, chefs and managers. There may be other chances to create new jobs as well. For example more visitors might mean there is a need for more:

✪ **Car park attendants**

✪ **Ice cream sellers**

✪ **Deck chair hirers**

✪ **Tour guides**

✪ **Taxi drivers**

✪ **Shop assistants**

An increase in the number of visitors will also mean there is a greater need for transport services. Some temporary jobs may be created in order to improve

An opportunity to create new employment

the roads so that they can take more traffic. The local transport service will need to run more frequently during the peak tourism season, so that some extra seasonal jobs might be created.

It is not just tourism jobs which may increase in number. As more people visit a destination and spend money in shops and on accommodation so the shop and hotel owners become more wealthy. They spend the extra money they earn in other shops and on things like leisure activities and home improvements. This spending can help to create jobs in shops, leisure centres and home improvement services such as plumbing, electrical repairs and glazing. This effect is called *the multiplier effect*.

Exercise 6.1

1   Make a list of some extra jobs which might be created in a destination if it had a large increase in the number of visitors arriving.

2   Divide these jobs into two groups:

Those you would count as tourism jobs, e.g. working in a hotel

Those you would count as jobs serving both tourists and others, e.g. shop assistants

3   Design a diagram or flow chart which shows how extra visitors leads to more jobs both in tourism and in other occupations.

Does tourism always solve employment problems in a destination?

Places where the usual forms of employment do not offer so many jobs as they used to have often seen tourism as a solution to their problems. For example areas where the majority of the population once worked in:

industry (e.g. mining, ship-building),

agriculture (e.g. dairy farming, fruit growing),

sometimes find that a decline in these businesses has meant a big increase in levels of unemployment.

Attempts to create a new tourism industry in these areas and to find jobs for people may come up against a number of problems:

✪ **Some of the jobs are only part time**

✪ **In many destinations the jobs are only seasonal**

✪ **Many of the jobs are low paid**

✪ **People who have worked in other occupations may think of tourism jobs as unskilled**

Part time work and unsocial hours

Some tourism jobs are part time. This is often because there is not a need for the services they provide all the time. For example:

✪ **A cafe in a seaside resort may employ extra staff at lunch times only because that is easily their most busy time of day**

✪ **A deck chair hire company may only be open on fine days and the owner may not wish to pay staff when it is wet**

✪ **A night club may employ extra security staff in the summer from late evening until they close**

The advantage of part time work for employers is that they only have to pay staff when they are actually needed. They can increase or reduce the number of people they have working for them at very short notice.

The disadvantage for employers is that it means their staff do not stay long and staff turnover is high. This means that more time and money has to be spent on training new people to do the job properly.

Another reason why there are many part time jobs in tourism is that facilities like hotels and entertainment centres have to have staff working outside normal office hours. For a large hotel this means 24 hours a day. It is difficult to cover all these times of the day with people working traditional working hours.

Some workers, such as kitchen staff, may split the hours they work into two shifts. This is because the greatest demand in the kitchen is at lunchtime and then again during the evening. People working a *split shift* may work over lunchtime, have a break in the afternoon, and return to complete their working day in the evening.

People working in transport operations, such as air cabin crew or ferry staff, will also have to match their hours of work to when air and ferry services depart, the lengths of the journeys, and the destinations they are travelling to and from.

Not everybody finds part time and shift work a disadvantage. Among those groups who might benefit from it are:

- ✪ **Families with young children who can work when the children are at school or in the evenings**

- ✪ **Students who can arrange their working hours away from the times they are involved in studying**

- ✪ **People trying to earn enough to finance other interests like travel, music performance or sports training**

Seasonal employment

Many tourist destinations are more popular in the summer season and receive fewer visitors at other times. Others may have wet seasons when the number of visitors are fewer. Some, like ski resorts, depend on good snow conditions to attract people.

Having a peak period, with seasons of medium demand on either side, may have a number of effects on a tourist destination:

- ✪ **Extra workers are hired during the peak season**

- ✪ **Unemployment rises during the low season**

- ✪ During the peak season workers from surrounding areas leave their normal occupations, such as agriculture, to work in tourism

- ✪ Local people may combine more than one job, e.g. farming and running a bed and breakfast

- ✪ In some countries job opportunities in traditional occupations may fall because they do not offer as much money as jobs in tourism

On second thoughts, I'll leave the mushy peas

Exercise 6.2

Examine the table below and then answer the following questions.

Month	Full time	Part time	Total
January	70	95	165
February	80	90	170
March	85	95	180
April	110	210	320
May	140	345	485
June	160	410	570
July	185	405	590
August	165	415	580
September	165	405	570
October	85	185	270
November	75	100	175
December	70	100	170

continued

continued

1 Which are the **four** busiest and the **four** quietest months in the resort, measured in terms of the number of tourism jobs which are created?

2 Is the increase in jobs during the summer months greater in full time employment or in part time employment?

3 If all of those people employed in the resort in July were still living there at Christmas, how many of them would either be unemployed or working in a non-tourism job?

4 Use computer software to help you to represent this table of information in graphical form, e.g. in a bar graph or a pie chart. Make sure your information is clearly labelled.

Earnings from tourism

Visitors to a destination usually spend money and some of this is passed on in different ways to the people who live there. Visitors spend money on accommodation, transport, food and entertainment. They also pay money to tour operators and travel agents for package holidays.

Whether tourism benefits a region or country financially depends on a number of different things:

- ✪ **Whether the extra money created by tourism is spent locally**

- ✪ **Whether local infrastructure (e.g. hotels, roads) can be improved to keep up with the extra demand from tourism**

- ✪ **Whether tourism and leisure facilities are owned by local people**

- ✪ **Whether demand for tourist attractions and facilities stays the same**

- ✪ **How the value of the local currency compares with the currency of the visitors**

- ✪ **How high local taxes are**

- ✪ **Whether other industries in the area are making a profit**

How tourism affects a country's national economy

There are four main ways in which the government of a country can benefit financially from tourism:

- ✪ **Because visiting tourists spend money during their stay**
- ✪ **Because the government raises taxes on things people buy (e.g. Value Added Tax, export duties)**
- ✪ **Because the government raises income tax from any extra tourism employees**
- ✪ **Because it may earn payments in foreign currencies which have a higher value than the local currency**

In countries like Britain, tourism is important in bringing income from overseas visitors. However the British spend more on holidays overseas than visitors spend in coming to Britain and so, in terms of tourism overall, more money goes out of the country than comes in. For this reason the British government is keen to encourage people in the UK to take domestic holidays.

Activity 6.1

1 Discuss some of the advantages for British people of taking a holiday in the UK rather than going overseas.

2 Think up three slogans which might be used to persuade them to do this.

3 Design a poster, using one of your slogans, for a campaign by the British government aimed at persuading more people to take holidays in their own country.

Tourism and the balance of payments

Nearly all countries earn money from abroad but also spend money overseas. Tourism brings in more money in Italy and Spain than the amount spent by

Spanish and Italian travellers overseas. The opposite is true in Holland and Germany, where visitors to the country spend less than the Dutch and Germans do on their travels outside their own countries.

It is very difficult to work out how much of the money spent by tourists from outside a country actually ends up in the local economy. Some of this money returns back overseas for reasons like these:

- ✪ **Hotels and restaurants import foreign food to suit the tourists**

- ✪ **Foreign equipment, materials and staff are used for new building and development work**

- ✪ **Hotels and facilities are owned by foreign companies who take the profits**

- ✪ **Payments have to be made to foreign companies, such as airlines**

- ✪ **To attract more visitors, money has to be spent advertising the destination country overseas**

- ✪ **Increased local incomes from tourism creates an increase in the importing of other foreign goods such as clothes**

The multiplier effect

In places where tourism increases, other industrial activities may also increase as a result of this. For example a growth in the number of tourists means an increased demand for food. This may encourage some local farmers to increase their production in order to sell it to local hotels and restaurants.

Other economic activities which may grow as a result of increased tourism are:

Building development

Road improvement

Setting up new telecommunications links

Developing sewage systems

Improving water and power supplies

The way in which money spent by tourists means that tourism employees earn more and spend it in a way which means that other local businesses grow is called the *multiplier effect*.

Exercise 6.3

1   List the things you spent money on the last time you went on holiday.

2   Design a flow chart or diagram to show how the money you spent may eventually have been spread among different parts of the local community.

Cultural impacts

Cuisine

Many tourists prefer to eat the same sort of food they have at home. This can cause problems for tourist destinations. For example:

- ✪ **They may have to import foreign foods which are more expensive**

- ✪ **Local restaurants may find it difficult to compete with new fast food outlets**

- ✪ **More expensive hotels may employ foreign chefs**

Tourism also introduces the local community to foreign foods. So, we find McDonalds and Burger King in many destinations outside North America. Brand names like Coca Cola are now available worldwide. However the influence on cuisine is not always one way. Travel may give people a taste for foreign food. It seems highly probable that there is a link between the growth of long haul holidays to Thailand and the increase in the number of Thai restaurants in Britain.

Food is not generally the main factor in choosing a destination, but, as the brochure extract below indicates, it is sometimes promoted as an important part of the whole holiday experience:

A taste of Tuscany and Umbria

When one thinks of Tuscan cuisine one thinks of olive oil and wine – certainly these two items are essential to the enjoyment of any Tuscan meal. The emphasis in Tuscany is on simplicity and restraint; meat is grilled and you will find spinach, beans and artichokes on every menu.

Extra virgin olive oil is the key to this cuisine and is also one reason why, whether you eat in a farmhouse or a five star hotel, there is a consistently delicious quality to the food. Umbrian cuisine takes its influences from Tuscany, with its roots in peasant cooking. However Umbrian food has one secret ingredient that transforms even the simplest dish into a meal fit for a king – *black truffles*, which you will find on every menu, in every restaurant. Olive oil is stronger here than in Tuscany, wines are superb and a delicious speciality is 'Porchetta' – roast pork stuffed with garlic and fennel.

Activity 6.2

1   Choose an overseas tourist destination and use cookery books in your school or public library to find descriptions of *three* dishes which are traditional there.

2   Design a page for a holiday brochure on which you try to show why the cuisine of this region is something that visitors would really enjoy.

Dress

In many cultures exposing the body is still thought of as shameful, but beach tourists do not always take notice of these feelings. They may wear very little clothing as they search for the perfect sun tan.

To prevent this issue causing conflict tourist destinations may:

✪   **Set up nudist beaches, some distance away from residential areas**

✪   **Place notices at exits from the beach, requesting that people should not enter the town in swimwear**

In many tourist destinations religion affects what is thought of as appropriate dress. Since religious buildings such as churches, cathedrals, monasteries and abbeys are magnets for visiting tourists, they are places where conflict can arise.

In many countries to enter religious buildings women must wear some form of head covering and clothing covering the legs to the knees; in some cases, arms and shoulders must be covered too. Men must wear long trousers and sleeved shirts.

In some destinations tourism may have increased interest in traditional forms of regional and national dress. Perhaps the presence of so many tourists, with their identical leisure wear, fosters a pride in the individuality of the kilt, the sari or the grass skirt. In many destinations, traditional costume has become an important feature of entertainments developed specifically to meet the demands of the tourist trade.

Exercise 6.4

1 Match the items of dress in Column **A** to the tourist destinations in Column **B**:

A	B
Fez	Texas, USA
Kilt	South America
Stetson	Egypt
Clogs	Scotland
Poncho	Holland

2 How might these items be used to encourage tourists to visit the destinations where they are worn?

Performance

Performances of music, dance and drama are often arranged specially to entertain parties of tourists.

These performances are usually based on local traditional culture but they are often changed from their original form.

Here are some of the problems which putting on some of these performances can bring:

Tour operators want performances every night

Dances and dramas may belong to specific festivals or religious events only taking place at a particular time of year

The original performances are often long and their meaning may be hard to explain

Tourists often attend cultural performances expecting to be entertained rather than wanting to know about the culture

There is economic pressure on the host community to provide what the tourists want. This leads to a tendency to cater for the average tourist who may prefer a carefully-timed, visually attractive, entertaining, relatively simple performance to a genuine show of native music, dance or drama.

Local culture displayed for tourists

Activity 6.3

1   Choose *one* of the following:

    a ceilidh; a Morris dance; a mediaeval mystery play; an eisteddfod; a maypole dance.

    Explain what it involves.

2   In what ways do you think the performance you have chosen might change if it was being put on mainly for the benefit of foreign tourists?

Arts and crafts

Many people like to buy things to remind them of their holidays. These souvenirs often take the form of handicrafts.

Local makers of handicrafts will try to make things which they think match the tourists' tastes. This means they often concentrate on:

Scenery and animals

Things which are colourful

Things which will fit easily into a suitcase

Things which are meant to look old or antique

Things which exaggerate what the local people, places and animals look like

The high demand for souvenirs can mean that cheap materials and quick methods are used to produce handicrafts which are poor quality imitations of the originals. These are sometimes called 'airport art'. Some people say that this means that some of the traditional skills in making things are lost because it is more profitable to make cheap imitations. However an increased demand by tourists for handicrafts can also mean that people in tourist destinations start to relearn old craft skills because they think it will help them to earn money.

Exercise 6.5

1 List the souvenirs which your class or group has brought back from past holidays and link each one with a place. Explain why you bought them.

2 Suggest different ways of classifying these souvenirs, e.g. by price, quality, attractiveness, usefulness, what they were made of, etc.

3 Apply these classifications to the souvenirs you listed in **1**.

4 Write a short report showing whether the classifications you applied in **3** support the views (i) that tourism encourages 'airport art' (ii) that tourism encourages people to learn craft skills.

Language

There are three main ways in which tourism can affect language habits and usage:

- ✪ **People employed in the tourism industry learn the languages of the tourists**

- ✪ **People in tourist destinations copy the languages of their visitors**

- ✪ **Social meetings between tourists and local people mean they may learn and exchange words from each others' languages**

Some destinations use the languages to help them promote tourism. For example, they might:

- ✪ **Put up road and direction signs in both the native language and the languages used by the majority of visitors**

- ✪ **Publish maps and guide books using both the native language and the main languages of the visitors**

- ✪ **Support courses in the native language for students and other study groups from overseas**

- ✪ **Encourage overseas tour operators to include a basic guide to or at least some useful phrases in the native language in their brochures**

Religion

Religion plays a part in encouraging people to visit tourist destinations. Temples, cathedrals, shrines, statues, religious relics and pilgrimages can all draw travellers from far and wide. Places like Mecca, Jerusalem, the Vatican City and Benares have been visited by religious believers for many centuries. However, in modern times holy places have become destinations for people whose main motives are not religious. Modern tourists are as likely to be interested in architecture, art or history as religion – or perhaps they may just be curious about other people's way of life.

If a cathedral begins to attract large numbers of tourists several questions arise:

What kind of wear and tear will the building suffer?

Is the building and its contents secure against theft or damage?

Does the presence of tourists interfere with the prayer and worship of the cathedral's daily users?

Religious sites can be tourist attractions – St Peter's, Rome

Will visitors dress and behave in an appropriate manner and avoid giving offence to local cathedral users?

Should the presence of tourists be exploited, by means of shops or requests for money, in order to raise revenue for the upkeep of the cathedral?

Should the cathedral admit tourists at any time or only during agreed hours?

Problems arise when the number of tourists becomes greater than the number of worshippers. More people, even among the local population, may then begin to see the cathedral as a museum-like facility housing religious art and statues. People who want to use it for worship may become angry at the way the use of the building is changing.

Table 6.1 shows some of the variety of religious beliefs to be found in destinations popular with tourists.

Destination	Main religious groups
Antigua	Anglican, Methodist, Moravian, Roman Catholic, Pentecostal, Baptist, Seventh Day Adventist
Cyprus	Greek Orthodox, with Muslim minority
The Gambia	Over 80% Muslim with the remainder holding either Christian or Animist beliefs
Hong Kong	Buddhist, Confucian, Taoist, with Christian and Muslim minorities
Morocco	predominantly Muslim with Jewish and Christian minorities. Morocco's population and culture stems from a cross section of origins including Berbers, Arabs, Moors and Jews
Thailand	the vast majority adhere to Theravada Buddhism, with Christian and Muslim minorities
Turkey	Muslim with a small Christian minority. Turkey is a secular state which guarantees freedom of worship to non-Muslims

Source: *World Travel Guide* (Columbus Press)

Table 6.1

Activity 6.4

1 Choose *one* of the religious faiths listed in Table 6.1 and use a reference library to find out what its basic beliefs are.

2 In a destination where the majority of the host population are followers of the religion you chose in **1**, what do you think might be causes of conflict with tourists arising as a result of these beliefs?

Environmental impacts

Landscape

Landscape is very important in attracting visitors to many tourist destinations. However, large numbers of visitors can have a harmful effect on the landscape they have come to see.

a Rivers, canals and lake shores are popular with walkers, boat users and people fishing.

b Woodlands offer peace and quiet and shade in hot weather. They are popular with walkers and those intersted in wildlife.

c Hills and mountains offer good views and interesting walks. They are popular with people who like peace and quiet.

d Beaches are popular for sun bathing, swimming and water sports. Clifftop walks offer attractive views.

Different landscapes that tourists seek

Four types of landscape which are especially popular with tourists are shown above.

These landscapes can be spoiled by tourism in a number of ways.

Coastlines

- ❂ **Building high rise concrete hotels and apartments along the front**

- ❂ **Not clearing up litter on the beach**

- ❂ **Putting untreated sewage into the sea**

Rivers and lakes

- ❂ **Oil from boat engines**

- ❂ **Erosion of the banks caused by waves from boats**

Hills and mountains

- ❂ **Soil erosion caused by too many walkers**

- ❂ **Damage caused by horse riding, motor cycles and mountain bikes**

Forests and woodlands

✪ **Walkers and trekkers taking wood for fires**

✪ **People removing plants and wild flowers**

Soil erosion

Soil erosion is one example of the damage tourists can cause to the landscape. It happens in a number of stages:

1   **The ground is in good condition, with a covering of grass.**

2   **People trample on the ground, especially footpaths and areas where food, information or good views are available.**

   The effect of this trampling is to form a gulley. Rain washes soil away. Some grass dies as more people walk on it. There are now fewer roots and the rest of the grass eventually dies or is washed away by rain.

3   **As more rainwater washes soil down the gulley, rocks underneath the soil begin to appear.**

4   **The rocky gulley becomes more difficult to walk in, so people begin to trample the grass on either side. In this way the area of erosion gets wider.**

Some types of tourism involve activities which may have a big effect on the landscape. These include:

   Skiing

   Golf

   Trekking

In ski resorts

✪ **Trees are cut down to make space for ski slopes**

✪ **Snow machines use up water supplies to make artificial snow**

✪ **Soil erosion and plant damage can be caused by skiing over muddy patches**

✪ **Earth and rocks are moved to reshape slopes, increasing the risk of avalanche damage**

✪ **Views are spoiled by pylons, ski lifts, avalanche shelters and cable cars**

The impact of tourists on the landscape

On golf courses

- ✪ Trees are cut down to make space for fairways
- ✪ Earth is moved to make car parks, roads, and to lay pipes and power lines
- ✪ Large quantities of water and herbicides are used to keep courses healthy
- ✪ Herbicides and fertilisers may drain off into water nearby

On trekking trails

- ✪ Rubbish is left and not collected by anyone
- ✪ Trees are cut down for firewood, causing more rock falls and landslides
- ✪ Forest fires are started
- ✪ Paths are eroded by heavy use
- ✪ Plants and wild flowers are removed

Activity 6.5

1   For each of the three activities listed above – skiing, golf, trekking – make a list of suggestions for lessening the harmful effects they have on the environment.

2   Write a letter to a tour operator specialising in one of these three types of holiday, asking them about their environmental policy.

3   Compare the answer you got with answers received by other members of your group.

4   Using examples from the replies your group received, write a short report in answer to the question:

How much do tour operators offering ski, golf or trekking holiday packages do to make sure they are not harming the environment?

Air and road

Road traffic

Tourists often use cars and aeroplanes to get them to and around their destinations. Both these forms of transport add to air pollution.

The centres of historic cities are where tourist traffic has the greatest effect on the quality of air. Many historic cities have taken action to reduce the amount of traffic in their centres. The main ways in which they have done this are:

✪ **Park-and-ride schemes**

✪ **Cycle routes**

✪ **Cheaper fares on public transport**

✪ **Stopping city centre parking**

✪ **Providing more coach parks**

✪ **Making pedestrianised areas**

✪ **Making signposted touring routes for motorists avoiding the city centre**

Reducing traffic in city centres

Air traffic

Aeroplanes burn a lot of fuel and, as a result, give off poisonous gases into the air. There has been a huge increase in the amount of air traffic in the last 20 years so this kind of pollution has grown. More air traffic means planes often have to circle major airports waiting to land.

Airlines answer their critics by saying:

- ✪ **More air pollution is caused by road traffic and industry**
- ✪ **Better engine design means less fuel is burnt nowadays**
- ✪ **Planes also use less fuel because they are built of lighter materials and because their shape allows them to move through the air more easily**

Water pollution

Tourism can cause or add to problems of water pollution.

In a developing tourist destination . . .	the sea may become polluted with untreated sewage.
In a lakeside area . . .	the banks may be eroded by waves caused by tourist boats.
Around tropical islands . . .	coral reefs may be damaged by tourist boats, divers or added pollution.
Along coastlines and at sea . . .	water is polluted by litter thrown overboard from ships.

Beaches

Tourists are less likely to visit a seaside resort if they think the seawater is polluted. In the UK tourist resorts can apply to have their beaches classified as Blue Flag beaches. To win this award they have to show that:

- ✪ **The seawater is very clean**
- ✪ **Toilets are available**
- ✪ **Life saving and first aid facilities are available**
- ✪ **The beaches are cleaned thoroughly and regularly**

It is not easy to win a Blue Flag award. In 1997 only 38 beaches in the UK were awarded a Blue Flag.

Beaches in the UK now have to meet standards set by the European Parliament. Twenty samples of seawater are taken and nineteen of these have to have above the agreed level of purity in order to meet these European standards.

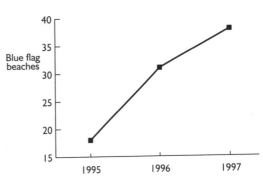

Activity 6.6

It would be possible to start a scheme like the Blue Flag award for *inland* areas of water which attract tourists.

1   As a group list as many *inland* tourist sites or destinations where water is a main part of the attraction as you can think of. Do not include indoor facilities, such as swimming pools.

2   Divide your list into groups (e.g. river sites, canals, lakes) and choose **one** of these groups.

3   Draw up a list of the kind of standards that you think this group of sites should be expected to meet in order to get an award.

4   Think of a suitable name for such a new award and discuss whether the places you have been to and the list you drew up in **1** would find it easy or difficult to achieve such an award.

Wildlife

Sometimes the growth of tourism can be a threat to wildlife. For example loggerhead turtles lay their eggs on the beaches of some Greek islands. A number of tourist activities can disturb the turtles' breeding habits. For example:

- ✪ **Motor boats and jet skis may stop the turtles coming ashore**
- ✪ **The turtles die as a result of eating plastic rubbish left on the beach**
- ✪ **The eggs are damaged by people digging in and riding vehicles over the sand**
- ✪ **Noise and lights upset the young turtles' sense of direction and stop them returning to the sea**

Here are six ways in which tourism can be a danger to wildlife:

Upsetting feeding and breeding habits

Hunting animals or vandalising the places they live in

Stopping animals entering their usual feeding grounds

Upsetting the balance between hunting animals and prey

Destroying feeding grounds so more animals are competing for less food

Feeding wildlife so that it becomes dependent on tourists

More animals competing for less food

More destinations are using wildlife as a way of attracting visitors. Examples include:

- ⊗ **Wildlife safaris, especially to see the African 'big five' (lion, leopard, elephant, rhino, water buffalo)**
- ⊗ **Galapagos Islands cruises to see rare birds and animals like the iguanas**
- ⊗ **Whale- and dolphin-watching cruises**

This kind of tourism can be a threat to wildlife. For example fast moving boats and light aircraft may frighten whales away from their traditional feeding grounds. However wildlife tourism also has to find ways to protect the wildlife which people come to see. There is a growing number of schemes to use some of the profits from wildlife tourism to find out what is needed to make sure rare birds, fish and animals can survive.

Wildlife can be used as a tourist attraction

Exercise 6.6

1   Make a list of some animals which used to live in the wild in Britain but which do not now.

2   Discuss some of the reasons why they might have died out.

3   Discuss which of these animals could be reintroduced into the wild and what sort of problems this might bring.

4   How could the reintroduction of these animals in a local area be linked to developing a new plan for wildlife tourism?

The built environment

The development of new tourist destinations usually means that new hotels and apartment blocks are built.

In many coastal areas, for example in parts of the Mediterranean, the type and quantity of such buildings has led to criticism. People have objected to:

- ✪ **Tall buildings along the edge of the beach which block the view**

- ✪ **Buildings which do not match the local traditional building styles**

- ✪ **Buildings which do not use local materials**

- ✪ **Buildings which are put up quickly and which soon begin to show signs of wear and tear**

- ✪ **Moving residents and businesses off their land in order to build on it**

- ✪ **The dirt, noise and nuisance caused by the building work**

The impact of tourism on the built environment

Tourism sometimes helps to conserve buildings. For example:

Ruined castles and country houses in need of repair have been restored and turned into tourist attractions, raising money for their owners by charging for admission

Old railway stations have been converted into museums and exhibition halls

Former warehouses and industrial buildings have been converted into craft centres and shopping centres

Former food markets, like Covent Garden, have been converted into shopping centres, cafes and restaurants attracting new visitors into the area

Change of use from food markets to retail tourism

Ribbon development

Tourism is often popular along coastlines, along river valleys and along scenic routes. This sometimes leads to building development along a narrow strip of land. There are a number of reasons for this:

- ✪ **People want to stay in hotels and apartments with the best views of the sea or other scenery**

- ✪ **They don't want to have to walk far to the main attractions**

- ✪ **In valleys or coastlines with mountains there is often only a narrow strip of land available for building**

- It is easier to deliver building materials to sites at the edge of a road

- Visitors are more likely to stop at accommodation and attractions which they pass on existing main roads

Planning permission

In most countries there are regulations to stop people from building anywhere. In Britain the Town and Country Planning Act (1946) means people have to apply for permission from their local council. Councils have to draw up local plans to say what the main uses of different areas should be, for example industrial, residential or leisure use.

People can object to new developments and, in the case of major developments like the development of Terminal 5 at Heathrow Airport, there may be a long inquiry before a final decision is made.

Activity 6.7

1 Collect some photographs or brochure pictures of hotels and apartments in a seaside resort you have visited.

2 List the main characteristics of these buildings, e.g. painted white – neon sign with hotel name on, etc.

3 If a developer was planning to build a new hotel or apartment block close to the ones you have pictures of, what regulations do you think the local council should insist on before giving them permission to build?

4 Prepare a wall display to show examples of good and bad hotel design.

Transport development

Tourism often increases the amount of transport used in and around destinations. For example:

- **Aeroplanes used to fly tourists there**

- **Cars, buses and taxis to take them to and from accommodation and places of interest**

- **Motor boats used for cruising and water sports**

Some tourist destinations were not built with modern transport systems. Their roads may be too narrow for tourist buses. New railway lines and new main roads may make it more difficult to get from the town to the beach. Airports built close to resorts may make them very noisy.

Table 6.2 shows some of the ways in which transport development in tourist destinations may cause environmental problems.

Type of transport	Problems caused
Aircraft	• Noise
	• Air pollution
Cars and buses	• Air pollution
	• Traffic congestion
	• Damage to road surfaces
	• Soil erosion caused by off-road driving
Railways	• Dirt and noise during construction of new lines
	• Spoiling of views by overhead cables

Table 6.2

However transport development can also benefit tourism, providing new and interesting ways of exploring the destination and the region around it.

Exercise 6.7

1 Choose one holiday which you have been on recently.

2 List all the types of transport you used in order to get there, to travel around while you were there and which you used for entertainment.

3 Draw a table like the example in the table below in which you list each of these forms of transport and note any ways in which you think they affected the environment.

4 Add a third column to the table and write in it any ways in which the harmful effects could have been reduced.

continued

continued

Form of transport	Possible environmental impact
Taxi to the airport	Exhaust fumes adding to air pollution
Aeroplane to Tobago	Exhaust fumes adding to air pollution
	Noise on landing over local houses
Cycling to beach	None
Motor boat trip	Noise affecting people on beach
	Oil polluting water
	Coral reef damage from anchor and passing over coral in shallow water

Noise and litter

Noise

As we have seen, the fact that tourism often leads to transport development also means it creates more noise. However, not all of this noise is caused by more aeroplanes or more cars. Other examples are:

- ✪ **The noise of crowds on beaches, or in popular countryside spots or in religious buildings like cathedrals**

- ✪ **The noise coming from music systems in bars, cafes, restaurants and discos**

- ✪ **The noise caused by leisure activities such as waterskiing**

Noise disturbance causes the greatest problems in tourist destinations when it lasts into the night and disturbs peoples' sleep.

Litter

Popular tourist destinations and attractions often have problems with litter. The main problems are:

- ✪ **Popular fast food and drinks are often supplied in brightly coloured packaging which is not easily destroyed**

Noise pollution

✪ **In new and small resorts there may not be an organised system of rubbish disposal, especially where the number of visitors is far higher than the number of local residents**

✪ **Cleaning up rubbish and preventing people from dropping litter is expensive in terms of notices, bins, equipment and people**

✪ **If litter is not removed it can, especially in hot countries, increase the risk of the spread of disease**

✪ **Cuts caused by metal and broken glass, especially on beaches**

✪ **Fires caused by throwing away cigarette ends**

✪ **Wildlife becoming ill as a result of feeding on human litter or packaging**

Activity 6.8

1   Visit a beauty spot in your area at a time in the year when it is likely to receive a lot of visitors.

2   Draw a sketch map of the area and mark the places where there are rubbish bins.

3   Mark on your sketch map the places where you see the greatest amount of litter.

4   Write a short report saying:

what are the main causes of litter at this site;

what might be done to reduce the amount of litter left.

Energy and water consumption

Large numbers of tourists staying in any destination means there is a need for extra energy to provide things like:

Heating

Air conditioning

Lighting

Hot water

Cooking facilities

In small towns there may only be limited supplies of electricity, gas, oil or coal and if this is used up by visitors there is not enough for local people. The same is true of water supplies, especially in hot, dry places where water shortages are common.

Tourist facilities like airports, hotels, attractions and sports facilities need good supplies of both energy and water in order to stay open.

In destinations where energy and water supplies are limited, it is important for tourist facilities to try and use as little energy and water as possible. Here are some ways they can do this:

- ✪ **Put in systems which turn lights out when people leave their rooms**
- ✪ **Cover swimming pools at night so they need less heating next day**
- ✪ **Use insulation to keep rooms, pipes and water tanks warm**
- ✪ **Only run washing machines on full loads**
- ✪ **Only provide hot water in the morning and evening**
- ✪ **Recycle waste water for use in watering plants**
- ✪ **Reduce washing by providing fresh towels on request only**
- ✪ **Train staff to save water and energy where possible**

Activity 6.9

You are the manager of a new hotel in a tourist destination where energy and water supplies are low.

1 List the ways in which you think water and energy use in the hotel could be limited.

2 Prepare a short talk which you will give to new employees, showing them how you expect them to help in saving water and energy supplies.

3 Prepare some overhead projections to use with your talk.

Changes in cultures, values and attitudes

Tourism may have an influence on the social behaviour of people in destinations where visitors come mainly from different cultures. The visitors may bring different attitudes and beliefs and these may be copied by local people, perhaps believing that people from richer countries must be more successful than they are.

This is often called *the demonstration effect*.

It is very difficult to measure this kind of tourism impact but examples of the way it happens include:

clothes	People give up traditional local dress and buy expensive foreign imports such as jeans
language	More English words are introduced into the local language
religion	People begin to think that their traditional beliefs are out of date
values	People change their behaviour, giving up traditional moral standards and beliefs
food	People prefer foreign fast foods to traditional dishes and cooking skills are lost
music and the arts	Western music and films become more popular than traditional local entertainments

This kind of tourism impact can lead to disagreements within the local community about the benefits or disadvantages of tourism. Such disagreements will often be strongest between older and younger generations.

However it may not be fair to blame tourism for these changes in values and attitudes. Many young people in tourist destinations will have been made aware of different beliefs in other countries through watching television, reading magazines or as a result of their own travelling.

Attitudes may also change as a result of watching television

Exercise 6.8

1   Write a conversation between a grandfather and a granddaughter living in a rapidly developing tourist destination. The grandfather is worried that tourists will introduce bad habits among local young people. The granddaughter thinks more visitors will bring a bit of excitement to the place.

2   What things do you think an older generation in a small village could do to try and make sure that tourism did not destroy what they thought of as traditional local values and beliefs?

Sustainable tourism

All industries have to think about their future. The tourism industry is growing very fast. In countries and regions where tourism is fairly new there is an added risk that tourism development will harm the environment so much that visitors will no longer be attracted to the area. If this happens the income from tourism in that destination will fall.

There are more and more examples of companies, governments and organisations with an interest in preserving the landscape working together to make sure that tourism can be sustained over a long period.

Sustainable tourism tries to benefit the local economy and the local people, while at the same time protecting the attractiveness of the place they live in. In other words it is about trying to find a balance between:

✪ **Allowing visitors to do and see what they want to**

✪ **Making sure this does not damage the place they are visiting**

✪ **Making sure the lives of the people who live there are not spoiled**

All of the following types of organisation can help by taking action to support sustainable tourism:

Tour operators

Travel agents

Hotels

Transport providers

Tourism associations

Government tourism offices

Table 6.3 shows some of the ways they can do this:

Tour operators	Hotels	Tourism associations
• Giving advice to travellers in brochures • Giving money to charities in destinations • Sponsoring research into the impact and management of tourism • Employing local tour guides	• Developing policies on recycling, waste management and use of power and water supplies • Working closely with local and regional governments • Using local produce • Employing local people	• Giving advice to members • Encouraging support from members to companies which actively support responsible tourism
Travel agents	**Transport providers**	**Government tourism offices**
• Using recycled paper • Providing specialist knowledge about responsible tourism	• Monitoring noise and fuel emissions • Providing advice for travellers cruising in environmentally sensitive areas	• Supporting research on the impact and management of tourism • Providing adequate infrastructure • Diversifying tourist attractions throughout the country

Table 6.3

Exercise 6.9

1   Choose one tourist destination where tourist numbers have grown very quickly in recent times.

2   For *each* of the six organisations in Table 6.3 above write a sentence showing how you think they could help to ensure that this destination is not spoiled by tourism.

Tourists themselves can also take responsibility for helping to protect the destinations they are attracted to. Here are some ways people who enjoy skiing can help to lessen the damage skiing can cause to the environment:

✪ **Only travel with tour operators who support conservation programmes**

✪ **Give some money towards tree-planting or other conservation projects in the destination**

✪ **Avoid areas which rely on artificial snow**

✪ **Don't ski when the snow is patchy – you will add to soil erosion**

✪ **Spend some of your time off the slopes, for example on cross-country skiing**

✪ **Only ski in areas which are marked off as suitable**

Pressure groups, such as Tourism Concern, help to draw the attention of governments, the tourism industry and the public to the harmful effects of tourism and to ways of reducing its negative impact.

The UK government's Department for International Development (DFID) picks out three key issues if tourism is going to be sustainable. The DFID says it is vital to make sure that:

Local communities play a role in tourism development and management – and gain a fair share of its benefits

Destinations receive long-term investment and commitment from tour operators – providing economic stability

The tourism industry plays a part in helping to conserve the aspects of destinations which made them attractive to visitors in the first place

Here are some ways in which local communities can play a part in tourism development and increase their direct earnings from it:

✪ **Supplying building materials**

✪ **Producing food**

✪ **Making furniture**

✪ **Selling arts and crafts**

✪ **Acting as guides**

✪ **Providing local transport services**

✪ **Providing low cost accommodation**

✪ **Putting on cultural exhibitions and shows**

(a)   *(b)*

A protected (a) and developed (b) tourist scene

Exercise 6.10

1   Look over all the Activities and Exercises you have completed in this chapter.

2   Construct a table with two columns in which you list all the possible benefits and all the possible drawbacks which might come with new tourism development

3   Write a short report suggesting some of the ways in which you think international tourism might change over the next 20 years.

Glossary

Word/phrase	Definition
bedspaces	a measurement showing the maximum number of people who can stay in a hotel or be accommodated in a region
charter flight	a flight booked for a special purpose such as taking holiday-makers to a particular destination
commission	a sum paid by a tour operator to a travel agent, usually a percentage of the value of each of the tour operator's holidays which the travel agent sells
conservation	protecting from damage and managing buildings, artefacts and landscape in such a way that they can be enjoyed by future generations
franchise	where one company pays to sell the products or services of another company or buys the right to use their brand name
labour intensive	a business operation which depends on a large number of staff to provide goods or services
multiplier effect	the way in which spending on one type of activity, such as tourism, also increases spending in other businesses, such as food shops
qualitative data	information collected from surveys and questionnaires which is more difficult to measure, e.g. levels of service, cleanliness
quantitative data	information collected from surveys and questionnaires which can be counted or measured
restoration	turning buildings, artefacts or landscape back to the condition they were in before they suffered from damage or wear and tear
room occupancy	a way of measuring how well a hotel is doing by working out the percentage of rooms occupied over a period of time
scheduled flight	a flight which runs according to an airline's regular timetable
sectors	different groups of similar businesses within an industry, e.g. the events sector within the tourism industry

Index

water 204–5
preservation 90
pricing holidays 66–9
principals 33–4
private sector 48, 50, 145
promotion 68, 138
publicity 138
public relations 138
public sector 48, 50, 145

qualifications 96, 169–71

railway buffet/restaurant car 28
rain 55
religion 197–9
resort couriers 176
resort representatives 39, 176
restaurant 26
restoration 75, 90
ribbon development 209
rivers and lakes 200
road traffic 203

safaris 207
sales promotion 138
schedule 142
sea bathing 73
seaside resorts 71–7
services 46–7
shopping centres and markets 91, 109
short breaks 87
short haul 38, 100–102
signposting 81
skiing 201, 218
skills 161–5
ski resorts 56–7
snow 56
souvenirs 114–16
special interest holidays 93–4
split shift 187
sports 95
sports and leisure centres 91, 120–146
    budget 124
    community 137–8
    demand 123
    events 140–4
    health and safety 134–6
    income and expenditure 124–5
    indoor facilities 121
    location 125
    management 127–8
    outdoor facilities 121
    prices 131–3
    promotion 138–9

staffing 129–30
sports and outdoor activities 43–5
stewards and stewardesses 176
sustainable tourism 217–20

taxation 190
teams 127
television 110, 216
temperature 54
tent 12
theatres 91, 119
theft 142
time differences 60
time zones 60
tourism industry 7–11
tourism jobs 184–5
tourist boards 49
tourist destinations 59–60
tourist information 103–6
Tourist Information Centre 46, 47, 91,
    104–6
tourists
    definition of 2
tour operators 33–4, 38–40
    domestic 38
    incoming 38
    jobs 156
    overseas 38
    specialist 38
tours 112–14
towns and cities 84–91
Town and Country Planning Act (1946)
    210
traffic congestion 87–9
training 96, 169–71
transport 16–25
    development 210–12
    links 20–3, 59, 62–3
    systems 16–19
    types of tourism transport 19–20
travel agents 33–4, 35–7
    jobs 156–7
travellers' cheques 45
trekking 202

unsocial hours 186

villa 12
voluntary sector 49–50, 145

water consumption 214–15
wildlife 77, 206–7
winds 54–5
working conditions 172–7